Mexican Art and the Academy of San Carlos, 1785–1915

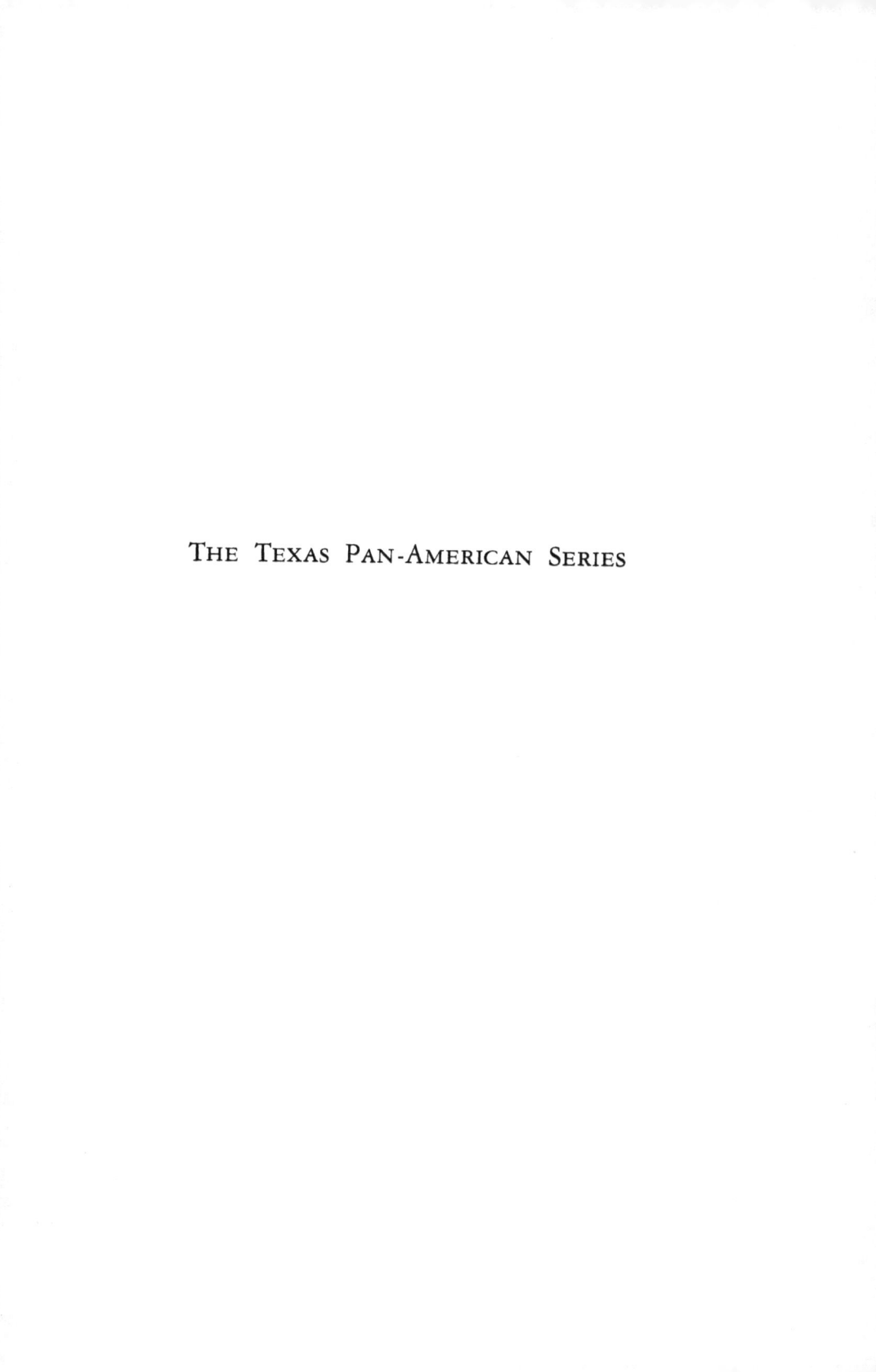

THE TEXAS PAN-AMERICAN SERIES

MEXICAN ART

and the ACADEMY OF SAN CARLOS

1785-1915

BY JEAN CHARLOT

FOREWORD BY ELIZABETH WILDER WEISMANN

UNIVERSITY OF TEXAS PRESS, AUSTIN

Library of Congress Catalog Card No. 61–13318

ISBN 978-0-292-74231-4

TO ANN

FOREWORD

IN THE ART OF MEXICO since the Spanish Conquest, it has been assumed that there are two periods, the Colonial and the Modern. Between these lustrous plateaus lay a dark hiatus called Neo-Classicism, dominated by the Academy of San Carlos, from which we have turned away our eyes in distress. Like a grandfather who was an embezzler, this period seemed not only to be unsuitable, but to have no connection with the family line. But along with our distrust of the autocratic and the derivative in art, we have today a special curiosity about the varieties of art, and the character of periods of transition. So we come to wonder what was really happening in

Mexican art while the country fought through one revolution after another to political independence.

This little text makes the first attempt to understand that episode, not by preconception or deduction, but by looking at the Academy itself. It is a straightforward, documented report of how things really were then. We are given not merely opinion and criticism, but evidence: the curricula, the drawings, the characters, the finances of the school. The archives have been there all the time in the Escuela Nacional de Bellas Artes; but no one thought about it until Jean Charlot (looking for something else) discovered their extent and interest.

The neo-classic period was everywhere rich with paradox. In the nineteenth century, academies were set up all over the Americas under the patronage of the governments. At once a school and a ministry of taste, the academy's strength lay in its absolute doctrine. Here the young artist was taught unequivocally what True Taste was; he was given the rules defining Beauty, and the techniques proper to the Fine Arts. By following the rules he was saved from vulgarity and, worst of all, provincialism. That the professors who came to Mexico or Rio de Janeiro knew nothing about Mexico or Brazil was not felt to be an impediment: they knew all about Art, and for that sublime, invariable, and artificial activity they had the perfect formula. The first great paradox is that such an esthetic could coincide with a period of revolution, from David in France through Thomas Jefferson in the United States and Tolsá in Mexico. A second paradox was that this authoritarian neoclassicism did become a popular form, not only because it was new and noble, but because it was philosophical and international: it offered a specific liberation from the Baroque tradition of the colony. The final paradox is in fact revolutionary, a complete reversal, since from the clean break with the old tradition a modern and national art could arise.

All of the philosophical conflicts of the period move in this story. Brave but insecure, rushing to demonstrate that they too were citizens of the world, that they knew as well as anyone what Culture was, the new nations were more colonial than the colony. But human nature remains stubbornly natural, and creative invention is perhaps more natural than obedience. Experience, personal and national experience, keeps breaking in; the charms of vulgar life and popular art keep tempting the artist to the expression of something fresh and genuine. Critics make the revolutionary discovery that the sculptors of Greece did not set out to produce Classic sculpture, but to realize their convictions about human destiny. The young Mexican painter, using his eyes, sees that he is walking in a world of men who are not put together by classical canons of proportion. It becomes clear that Moctezuma's costume, his face, his figure, and his way of moving cannot be deduced from the ruins of Rome or even Egypt, and that these differences are indeed the cardinal interest of the Aztec Emperor. Life is bulging with half-realized significance, which is relevant to this time and place, and it is the business of the artist to bear witness to what he has seen.

It is precisely at this point that *americanismo* is born. Foolish as esthetic doctrine, it is still the attitude that liberates the native artist from foreign domination: the artistic declaration of independence. There is nothing more sure than that a painter should paint what he sees and knows, and inasmuch as he is a Mexican, it will be a Mexican story that he tells. So in the end the struggle was drawn in Mexico between classical tradition and the necessity of making a new art for themselves, and it was this choice that was fought out in the Academia de San Carlos in New Spain between 1785 and 1915.

Like everything in Mexico, the conflict is wonderfully overt, a reduction to essentials, almost under laboratory conditions, of the complex elements of cultural growth. It is a running battle

11

between the Academy and chaos, in which the moments of worst confusion are in fact the most pregnant. The documents voice with simplicity the assumptions which establish the plot and motivate the actors. What is most interesting in the record is that there were always unregenerate elements at hand, ready to take over when official force weakened. And, as always in Mexico, what might be thought a peripheral conflict in matters of taste is in fact at the heart of national history. The change in the Academy was effected by the great political and sociological tides of the times: the forces which destroyed it also describe the fallacy of an art which disregarded them.

ELIZABETH WILDER WEISMANN

THE CONTENTS

THE ILLUSTRATIONS

Mexican Art and the Academy of San Carlos, 1785–1915

THE BEGINNINGS

THE Royal Academy of San Carlos in New Spain, chartered in 1785, is still in existence, though under another name and drastically modified in its approach. Within this long span of time it has lived through bewildering shifts in political fashions, coddled at times and at times snubbed by the swift succession of Mexican kings, emperors, dictators, and presidents. Today the old Academy is split into a school of architecture and a school of fine arts.

The Academy inherited at birth the policies, students, and director of its prototype—the school of casting and engraving of Don Jerónimo Antonio Gil—and some of the aims, records, and professors of the still earlier, short-lived private academy of painter Miguel Cabrera. Such continuity makes it possible to follow without substantial interruption the changing modes of art instruction in Mexico, from the middle of the eighteenth century to our day.

The twin schools—the School of Architecture and the School of Fine Arts—born of the ancient Academy are still quartered in the building that housed it in the 1700's—known previously as the Hospital del Amor de Dios—and data concerning the operation and personnel of the school have accumulated undisturbed through the wars for independence, more than a score of revolutions, and as many foreign invasions. These preserved documents form an authentic index to the shifts of taste in Mexico for two centuries, for even the somewhat static official art that it was the Academy's responsibility to guard and to foster remained subject to stylistic oscillations bred by periods and personalities.

The present relation, besides recounting some of the circumstances attending the beginnings of the school, follows up the story through the first fifteen years of the twentieth century. It is the first attempt ever made to synchronize papers in the school archives, many of them unpublished, with another set of papers that bear even more directly on matters of taste and style: the portfolios of original drawings preserved in the library of the Academy under the zealous care of Don Lino Picaseño. These are mostly charcoal renderings on large-sized sheets, an accumulation of yearly crops of teachers' models and students' prize-winners that cover in a practically continuous sequence the years from 1763 to 1915.

Jerónimo Antonio Gil landed in Mexico in 1778. Master engraver to the Spanish King, he was sent to the rich colony to supervise the art standards and metal-casting craft of its mint,

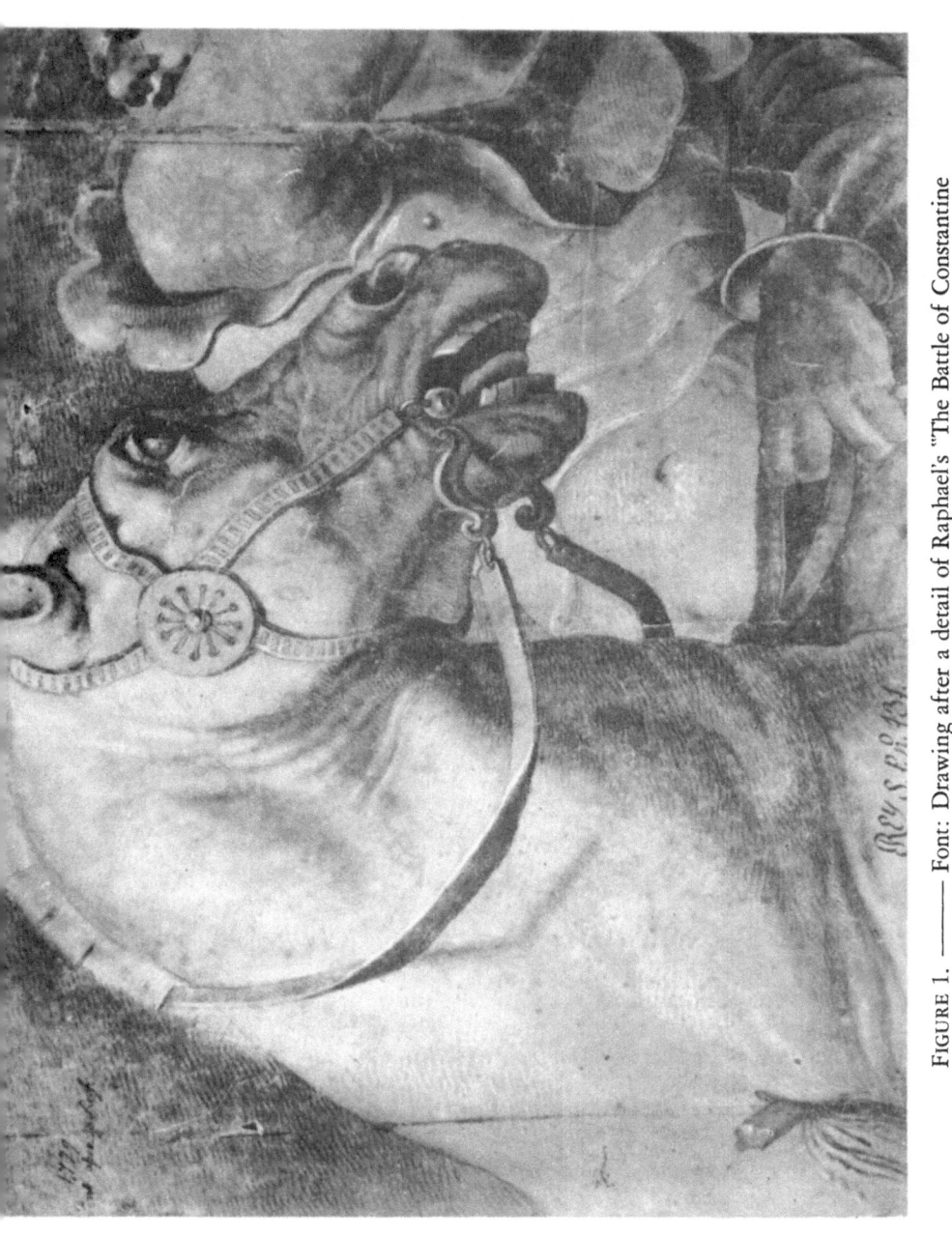

FIGURE 1. ——— FONT: Drawing after a detail of Raphael's "The Battle of Constantine against Maxentius," Vatican fresco. Chalk and charcoal on blue paper. Dated 1779. (Photograph by Lola Alvarez Bravo.)

or Casa de Moneda. The imposing building of the Royal Mint, with its arched tiers of corridors opening on a vast roofless patio, is now known as the National Museum of Archeology, but the street it fronts retains the name of Calle de la Moneda.

With an eye to training helpers in the intricacies of low-relief modeling and the casting of metals, Gil, whose official title was Tallador Mayor de la Real Casa de Moneda de México,[1] opened a school of engraving on the precincts. Besides engraving with burin as we commonly understand the term, he also taught *grabado en hueco,* that is, the art of making casting dies. The first students of the little school were three pensioners already provided for by the mint, and the two sons of Gil, Gabriel and Manuel.[2]

Figure 1 is a reproduction of a student drawing dated 1779, the first year that Gil taught. It is a copy of Raphael by a student named Font, in chalk and charcoal on blue paper. The downed and snorting horse and its rider, whose upraised arm is attempting to ward off an enemy blow, are rendered in a system of open hatching, with swelling and thinning lines, ultimately descended from the burin technique of the celebrated crafts-man Hendrik Goltzius. The specialized directives that engraver Gil gave his students are also evidenced in another drawing (Fig. 2) that dates of the time of transition between the engraving school and the Royal Academy. The subject matter appears to be a Carthusian monk in ecstacy. So perfect is the

[1] See the correspondence published in Genaro Estrada, *Algunos papeles para la historia de las bellas artes en México* (México, 1933), especially p. 12. Cited hereinafter as *Algunos papeles.*

[2] Abelardo Carillo y Gariel, *Datos sobre la Academia de San Carlos de Nueva España. El arte en México de 1781 a 1863* (México, 1939), p. 8. Cited hereinafter as *Datos . . ..* The baptismal names of the sons of Gil are taken from documents relating to the show of students' works which the Academy of Mexico sent to that of Madrid in 1796.—Estrada, *Algunos papeles,* p. 67.

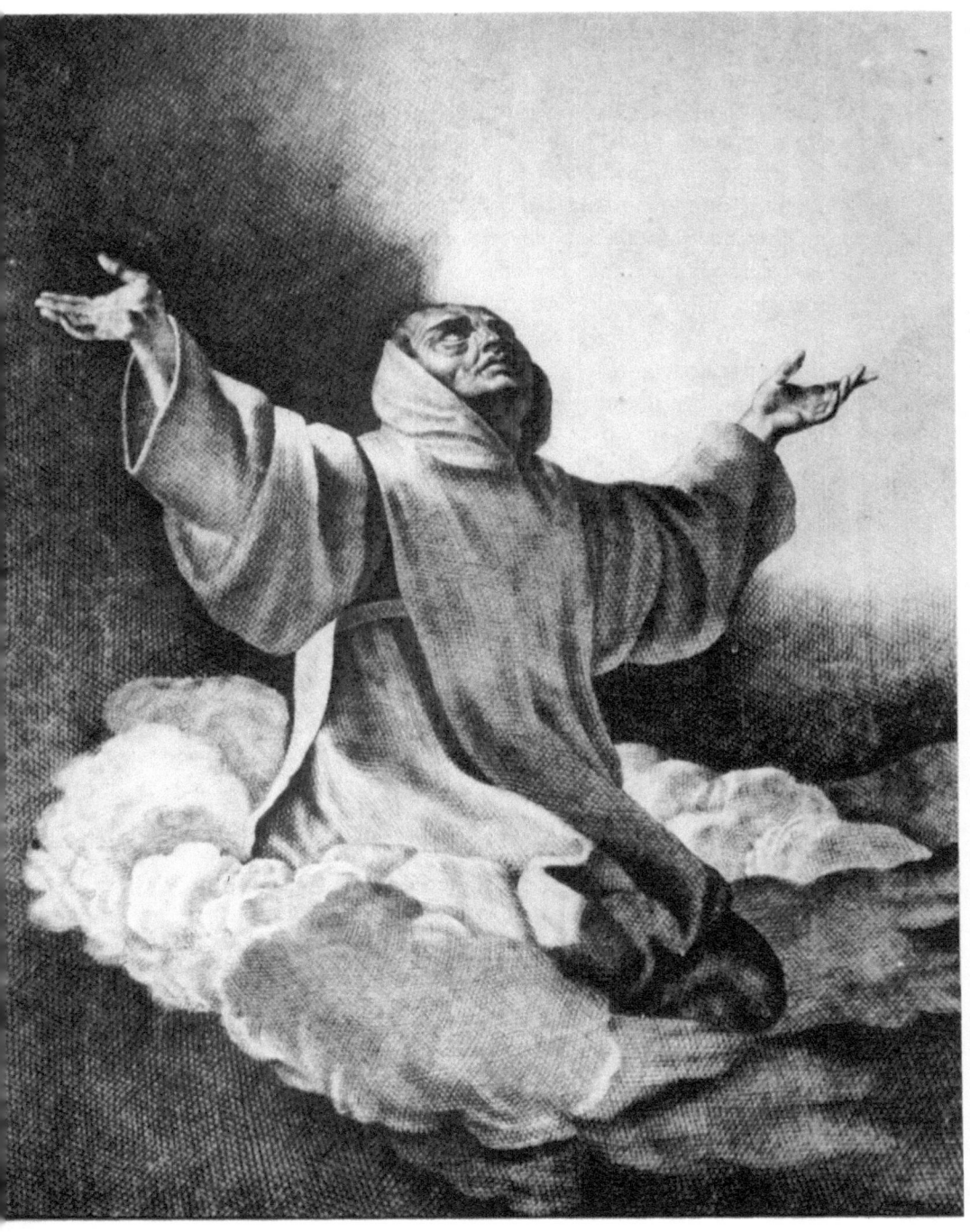

FIGURE 2. Julián Marchena: A Carthusian monk in ecstasy. Drawing in imitation of an engraving. Ink and wash. Captioned "Julian Marchena drew it at the age of fifteen under the guidance of Don Geronimo Antonio Gil. Year of 1785." (Photograph by Lola Alvarez Bravo.)

imitation of burin work as to amount to a steal. The young artist proudly captioned his make-believe engraving, "Julian Marchena drew it at the age of fifteen, under the guidance of Don Geronimo Antonio Gil. Year of 1785." Gil seems to have reciprocated Marchena's devotion. He followed his student's career long after the growing cares of his directorship had forced him to give up teaching Marchena personally. In a report dated 1790, which smacks of professional jealousy against the newly-arrived teacher of engraving, Joaquín Fabregat, Gil states how the newcomer keeps Marchena and another student in virtual slavery:

He makes them run the press [*tirar el tórculo*] when this type of work is proper only for menials [*cargadores*]. So employed, they lose both their pulse and their health. He forces them to pull editions of whatever works he makes, to his profit, while the students have only the work, without any benefit.[3]

In August, 1781, the first move toward transforming the school of engraving into a Royal Academy was made before the viceroy, Don Matías de Gálvez, by Don Fernando José Mangino, in charge of the Casa de Moneda and the direct superior of Gil. The engraving school was modified into a School of Fine Arts, or Escuela Provisional, and functioned in the same Casa de Moneda. The project was to reach full maturity with the authorized printing of the Statutes of the Academy, off the press just in time for their distribution to the many bigwigs, laic and ecclesiastic, who attended the inauguration of the newly-enlarged school on November 4, 1785. Thus at the inauguration a part of the ceremony was, paradoxically, a distribution of prizes to the most deserving students for work done during the past school year.[4]

[3] Carillo y Gariel, *Datos* . . ., p. 68.
[4] Diego Angulo Iñiguez, "La Academia de Bellas Artes de Méjico y sus

24

The Beginnings

As director of the Academy, Gil, in addition to the teaching of engraving, supervised also that of sculpture, painting, and architecture. A drawing (Fig. 3) that he made as a model for his students is dated of the next decade, 1794. One gets the feeling that in this chalk-and-charcoal rendering from life the engraver's exacting hand has consciously, if cautiously, loosened up in an effort to meet the broader requirements.[5]

The curriculum of the Academy followed the pattern set by European academies, where drawing was considered the common denominator of all the plastic arts; the student started by copying two-dimensional models, engravings, or original drawings made for the purpose by his teachers.

All that present themselves in the classroom where rudiments are taught shall be admitted, be it their purpose to specialize eventually in any one of the three arts, or engraving; or else to learn only drawing, so as to perfect themselves later in some other office.

At the monthly Board meetings are shown drawings by students who have progressed sufficiently . . . and want to pass, or are deemed worthy to pass, to another classroom. . . . Said drawings having been judged by a plurality of votes of the teachers to whose

Pinturas Españolas," in *Arte en América y Filipinas* (Sevilla, 1935), Vol. I, p. 1. Quoted by Carillo y Gariel, *Datos . . .,* pp. 12–13. Iñiguez' work is cited hereinafter as "La Academia de Bellas Artes." I mention here only the first and last events in the founding of the Academy, a period already well covered. For one of the more concise accounts, see Jesús Galindo y Villa, *Anales de la Academia Nacional de Bellas Artes de México* (México, Imprenta del Museo Nacional de Arqueología, Historia y Etnología, 1913), No. 1. Cited hereinafter as *Anales de la Academia Nacional.* Only the first number of this promising bulletin was published.

[5] A similar drawing by Gil, dated of that same year, and representing a man, seated and seen from the back, exists in the Academy files.—Justino Fernández, *El Arte Moderno en México, Breve Historia. Siglos XIX y XX* (México, Antigua Librería Robredo, 1937), Fig. 26. Cited hereinafter as *Arte Moderno.*

profession the student is inclined, it is decided if he should pass to the classroom where plaster casts are studied. . . .

To life class are admitted those who have followed a course parallel to that necessary for admission to the model class, the Board having declared them fit to pass.[6]

It is easy to scorn the rigidity of such a system when we compare it with the *laissez faire* that prevails in most art schools today, but some of the provisions, as stated by the King, point up in turn our own laxness in emphasizing the fundamental unity of all the arts:

So that the study of Architecture may proceed to the desired perfection, and so that all other arts and offices may receive the help that Mathematics should give them, it is my will that there be in the Academy two Directors of Mathematics and two of Architecture to teach these matters extensively. . . . Between them they must perpetually give and explain a most complete and methodical course of

---

[6] *Estatutos de la Real Academia de San Carlos de Nueva España.* En la Imprenta Nueva Mexicana de Don Felipe de Zúñiga y Ontiveros, Año de 1785, pp. 35–36, Statute 18, "Discípulos." The Statutes (p. 72) carry a short explanation concerning their distribution and the size of the edition: "The Secretary of the Academy shall cause to be made a certified copy of these Statutes. They shall be printed at the expense of the School, in as many copies as shall be deemed necessary, to be distributed among the Presidents and Trustees. Special copies shall reach the Royal Court of Appeals and other Courts of this capital, to be understood and observed as regards their office. Other copies are to be presented to the Very Reverend Archbishop and to the Bishops of New Spain, to the Tribunals, both ecclesiastical and secular, and eventually should reach all judges in the Kingdom, to be made known to all, each in his jurisdiction." Given also (p. 71) is the legal reason for the publication: "As concerns the printed copies (of these statutes), once certified by the Secretary of the Academy, they shall have the same validity and carry the same credence as the original." The copy that I use is duly certified in the handwriting of the first Secretary of the Academy: "Es copia de su original, de que certifico. México 19 de 8bre de 1785. Anto. Piñeiro." The statutes are cited hereinafter as *Estatutos.*

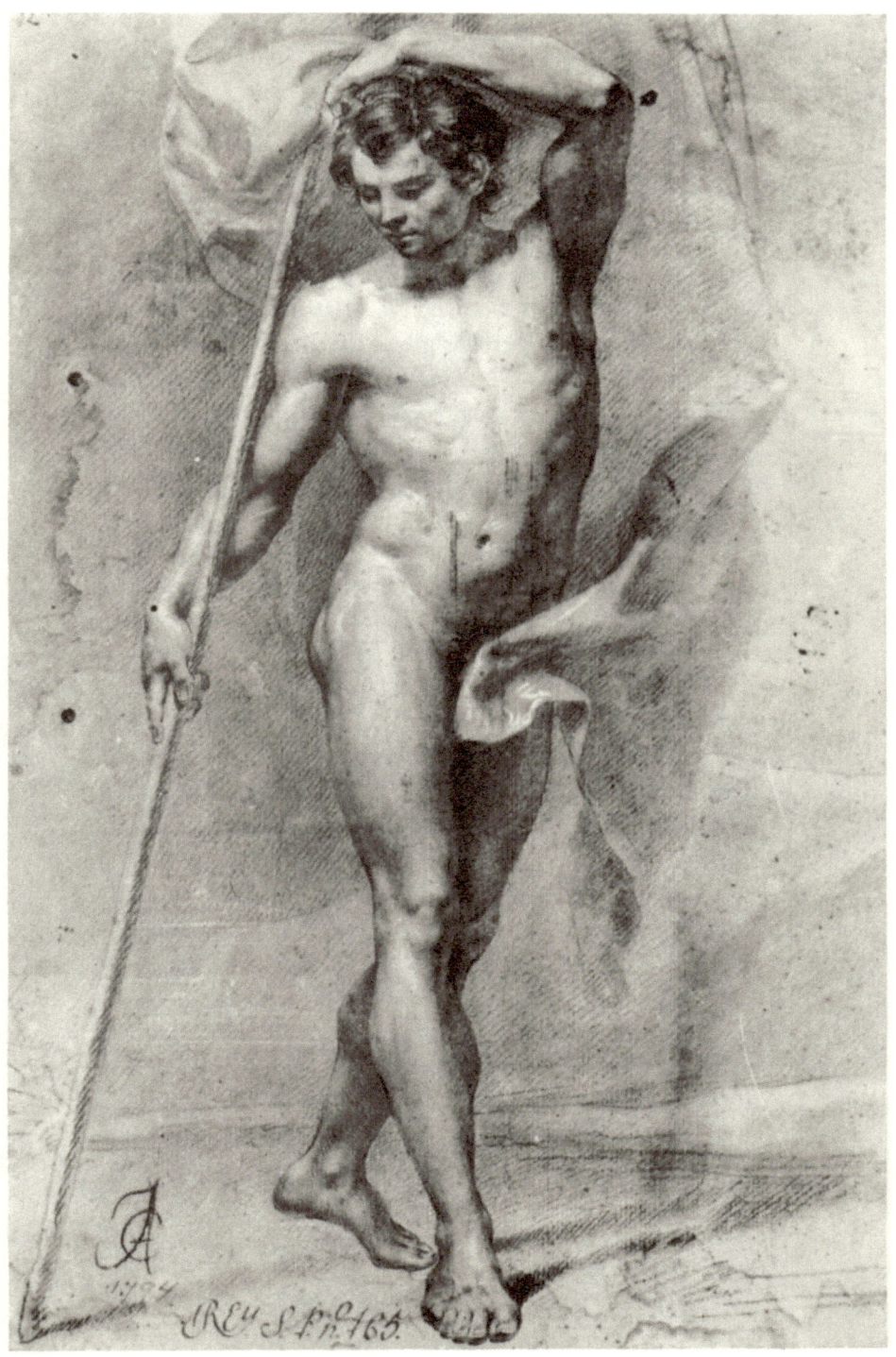

FIGURE 3. Jerónimo Antonio Gil: Life drawing done as a model for his students. Chalk and charcoal on tinted paper. Signed with his monogram, JAG. Dated 1794. (Photograph by Lola Alvarez Bravo.)

Mathematics and Architecture so as to perfect these studies and minister all possible light to other arts.[7]

In his new position, Gil proved a hard taskmaster, and he could well afford to bully his faculty. As the King phrased it: "The post of General Director is given for three years; the only exception to this rule is the present Don Jerónimo Antonio Gil, for, in consideration of his special merit, his being the first, and his role in the founding of the Academy, it is my wish that he serve in this post for his lifetime, a grace never to be duplicated in another."[8]

In the portrait of Gil (Fig. 4) preserved in the galleries of the Academy, painter Ximeno y Planes has scattered clues to the taste and the profession of the sitter. The powdered wig, Nattier blue coat, embroidered silk vest, and fine lace cuffs robe with authority the artist who could raise other artists to the coveted status of Academicians. This finery contrasts with the angry bulldog features, and eyes that focus straight at the onlooker, minus approval. Accessories bespeak the self-made man's achievements: an engraver's press embossed with the Royal Arms, engraver's burins, a die held in one hand and in the other the medal struck from it. In the background, a plaster cast of a head from the Laocoön group is a reminder that drawing was deemed the key to both painting and sculpture. Most importantly, the right fist weighted with the metal die rests possessively on a thin book, parchment-bound, its title prominently displayed on the spine: "E⁵⁻ D.L.R. ACADEM. D.S. CAR.D.N.E."—the hard-won statutes of the school.

In the interim needed to select and bring from overseas men already trained in the specialized methods of the Spanish acade-

---

[7] *Estatutos,* Statute 10, "Directores de Arquitectura y Matemáticas," pp. 25–26.

[8] *Ibid.,* Statute 27, "Elección y Duración de Oficios," p. 59.

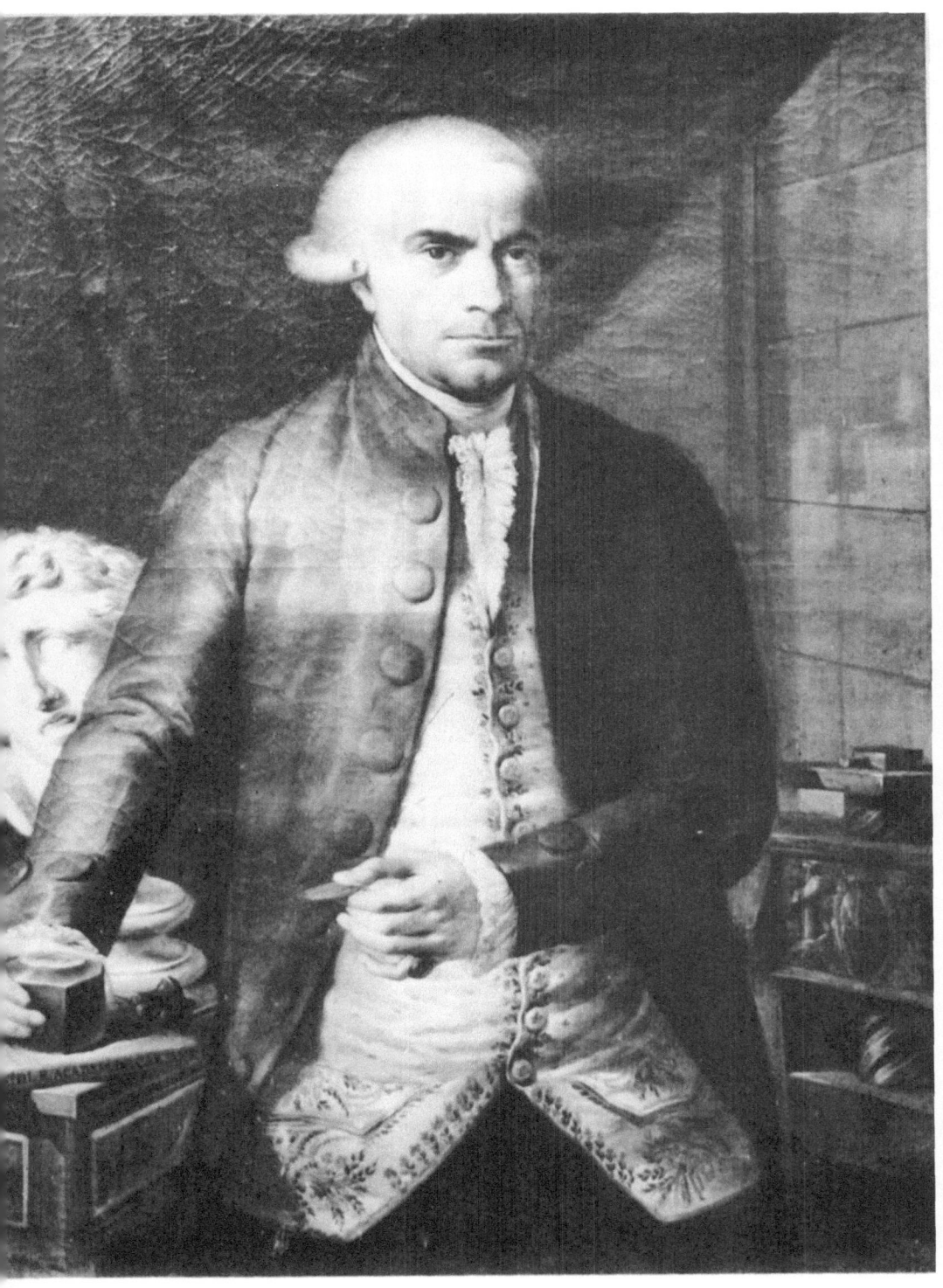

FIGURE 4. Rafael Ximeno y Planes: Portrait of Jerónimo Antonio Gil, founder and first director of the Academy. Galleries of the Academy. (Negative by courtesy of Juan M. Pacheco. Print by Gaud Foto.)

mies, Gil found it expedient to use for a temporary faculty Creole painters born and bred in Mexico, who were still proficient in the somewhat brittle graces that characterized most of their century. Now that the frigidity of Mengs was all the fashion in Madrid, this rococo manner was considered passé. Gil's executive coldness toward the Mexican artists underlined this fact, and helped to impress upon them that they were being used merely as stopgaps. A directorial report saw the following passage deleted before it reached its intended recipient, the viceroy:

. . . there have been many difficulties. For example, they tell me that, were they from Spain, their fate would be different; but, because they are Creole, they remain unappreciated and trod upon. It is taken for granted in Mexico that the Academy refuses to take interest in them, which arouses quite some criticism.[9]

Even after the arrival of the new faculty from Spain, some of the Mexicans retained their posts, among them Joseph de Alzíbar, a seasoned painter already well-known in the 1750's. A drawing of his (Fig. 5), done on yellow paper and dated 1796, justifies this venerable man's impatience as he faced official discrimination against native artists. The style of this charcoal and chalk rendering is fully mature; the dynamic chalk rendering of the arm in motion is stated with a simplicity superior in its breadth to the guile of Gil's neat engraver's line.[10]

[9] Quoted in Carillo y Gariel, *Datos . . .*, p. 16.

[10] The quality of Alzíbar's Academy drawing fully corroborates the opinion expressed by Manuel Toussaint that the two paintings published by Agustín Velázquez Chávez as by Alzíbar could not possibly be from his hand.—Agustín Velázquez Chávez, *Tres Siglos de pintura Colonial Méxicana . . .* (México, Editorial Polis, 1939), Plates 97, 98. For the critical estimate by Toussaint, see *Anales del Instituto de Investigaciones Estéticas,* No. 4, p. 67.

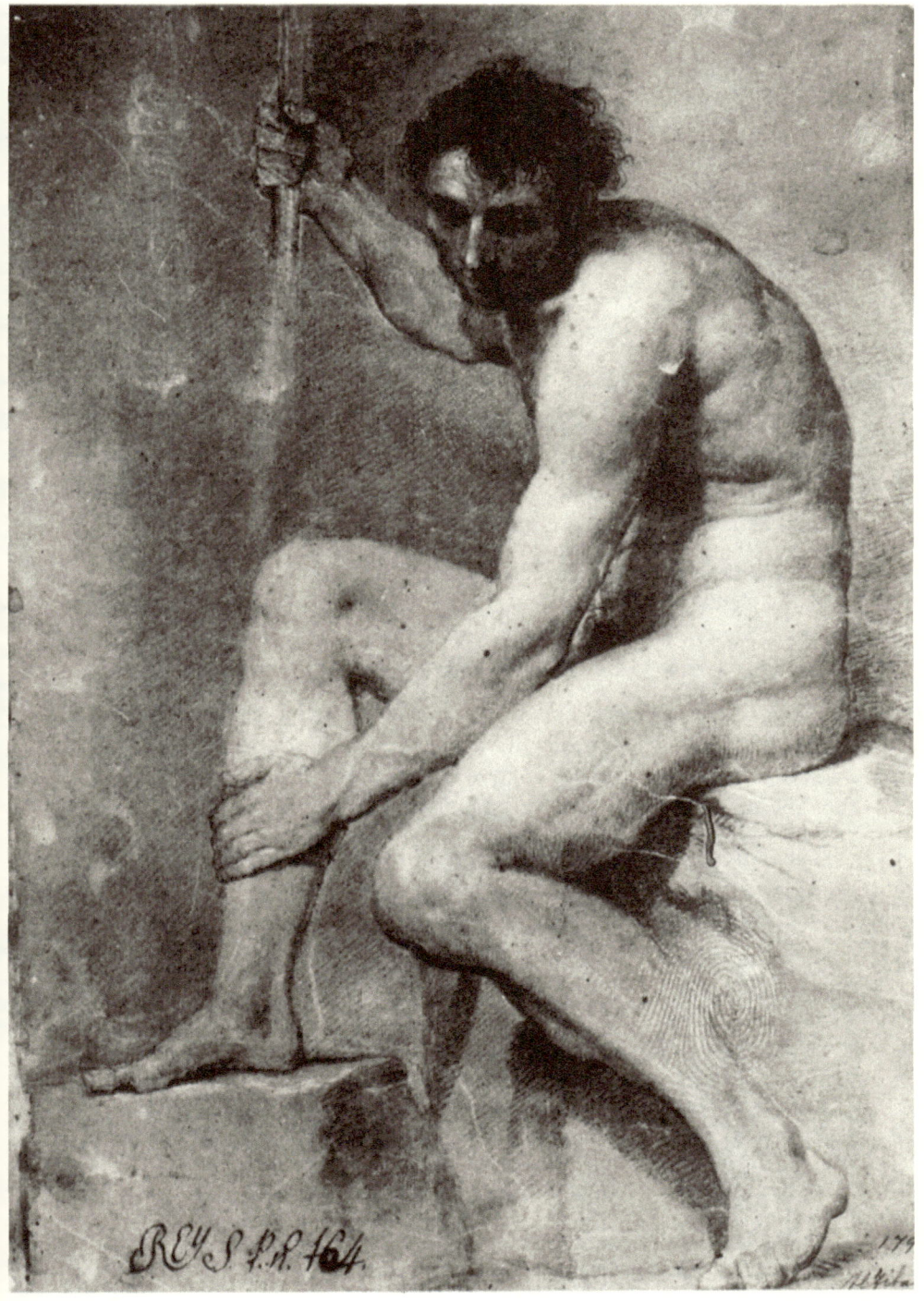

FIGURE 5. Joseph de Alzíbar: Life drawing. Charcoal, chalk, and ink on yellow paper. Dated 1796. (Photograph by Lola Alvarez Bravo.)

An intimate light on Alzíbar the man is shed by a passage in a letter that he wrote, dated September 17, 1756, to painter Miguel Cabrera, author of a book describing the miraculous image of Our Lady of Guadalupe.[11] Alzíbar's letter is the fifth in a set of opinions by well-known artists, commending the book and published as an appendix under the caption "Commentaries concerning this work, expressed by the professors of the Most Noble Art of Painting of the City of Mexico." With some originality in punctuation that is typical of the period rather than a shortcoming of the writer, Alzíbar reveals himself as a man of deep feelings and few words:

Yo confiesso con toda ingenuidad, aunque haga publica mi ineptitud, que desde, que vi esta celestial pintura quede tan admirado, que nunca pude explicar, lo que havia visto; y assi mi mayor expression, quando he sido, preguntado ha sido decir, que no se puede explicar.

(In all simplicity, even though it makes obvious my ineptitude, I admit that, from the moment I saw this heavenly picture, my awe was such that I could never analyze what it was I had seen. Asked for my opinion, I can only say that I have no explanation.)

Alzíbar lived long; he was still active in the first decade of the nineteenth century. José Bernardo Couto, writing in 1860, appraised Alzíbar as "the last of our painters of note. With him, the ancient Mexican School begun by Balthazar de Echave comes to an end."[12]

---

[11] Published by Miguel Cabrera in his *Maravilla Americana y conjunto de raras maravillas observadas con la dirección de las reglas de el Arte de la Pintura en la prodigiosa imagen de Nuestra Sra. de Guadalupe de México* . . . En México en la Imprenta del Real, y más antiguo Colegio de San Ildefonso, 1756. I quote from the facsimile edition, printed in Queretaro, Ediciones Cimatario, 1945. Cited hereinafter as *Maravilla Americana.*

[12] *Diálogo sobre la historia de la pintura en México* (México, 1872). Throughout, I shall quote from the reimpression of 1947 in *Biblioteca*

The Beginnings

In 1786, the imported faculty members landed at last from Spain. Their training had taken place mostly at the Academy of San Fernando in Madrid. The attempt to re-root them in New Spain was to prove a near failure, partly because Gil, entrenched in a lifetime post, was unbending even to his countrymen. The Statutes did indeed give the General Director wide police powers:

He shall always be given first place in all classrooms by the local director and assistants. He may make to anyone whatever admonitions and suggestions concerning studies he deems beneficial, always with politeness and moderation, and avoiding calling attention to the correction when possible.

If anyone fails to obey him, or commits a breach of modesty, or fails in other ways that, in his prudence, he believes to call for a stiff correction, he may reprimand the guilty one and even incarcerate him in the Academy building, and that not only when the delinquent is a menial, a student, or a Fellow, but also if he is an Academician of Merit, an Assistant, or a Director in function. . . .[13]

Going even further than the letter suggested, Gil forbade faculty members to accept any paid commissions without his consent, even though these be executed outside teaching time.

Problems of art added to the frictions of discipline. Never could Gil shed convincingly the engraver's specialized approach, to the disgust of the two new directors of painting, both practicing painters, Don Cosme de Acuña y Troncoso and Don Ginés de Andrés y de Aguirre. Acuña was in truth a mediocre artist, and his one drawing preserved at the Academy is of indifferent quality. Yet, in it, the painterly approach is clearly

Americana. Edición, prólogo y notas de Manuel Toussaint (Mexico–Buenos Aires, Fondo de Cultura Económica), p. 107. This work is cited hereinafter as *Diálogo.*

[13] *Estatutos,* Statute 7, pars. 2–3, pp. 21–22.

emphasized by the use of very coarse hatchings, done with purposely disordered strokes. This drawing illustrates the violence of Acuña's personal reaction to Gil's neat style.

Andrés was a better artist, and he did not need resort to exaggeration to press a point. His drawing after Mengs, dated 1794, of a male model holding his foot (Fig. 6), is a remarkably free performance, even touched with greatness. Looking at this sheet, one regrets all the more the loss of Andrés' only Mexican mural, painted on the vault of the baptistry of the Sagrario Metropolitano, and destroyed in the nineteenth century.[14]

The clash latent in the diversity of esthetic concepts is corroborated by the written plea that the disillusioned teachers, in a concerted bid for relief, sent in 1788 to the secretary of the

[14] Manuel G. Revilla mentions Andrés' dome as one of three Mexican precedents for Clavé's own mural work in the dome of La Profesa.—*Obras* (Agüeros, 1908), Vol. V, p. 184. Couto, however, quite a connoisseur, stated in 1860 in his *Diálogo* that he had seen only one painting by Andrés, a small Madonna of indifferent quality. José María Marroquí, in the posthumous edition of his *La Ciudad de México . . .,* describes the Andrés mural, but attributes it to an Italian painter: "In the pendentives of the dome of the baptistry, four baptismal scenes were painted in fresco, one of them the Baptism of Our Lord. They were painted by an Italian soon after the Sagrario chapel was built, and he received 500 pesos for each." A footnote gives the time of its destruction: "Not long ago, Father Paredes, the curate, had them whitewashed because of their dilapidated condition, and had the baptistry decorated in modern style.—(México, Tip. y Lit. "La Europea," de J. Aguilar Vera y Cía., 1900), Vol. III, p. 579. Perhaps this ignorance of the true authorship of the mural already dates from the time when Couto was gathering material toward the *Diálogo,* and explains how he failed to list to Andrés' credit such a conspicuous achievement. That Andrés painted this mural rests now on the word of Revilla, who did not name his source. It appears quite probable that Andrés did, however, as he had already painted frescoes in Spain.—Thieme-Becker, *Allgemeines Lexikon* (Leipzig, Verlag Von Wilhelm Engelmann, 1907), Vol. I, p. 140.

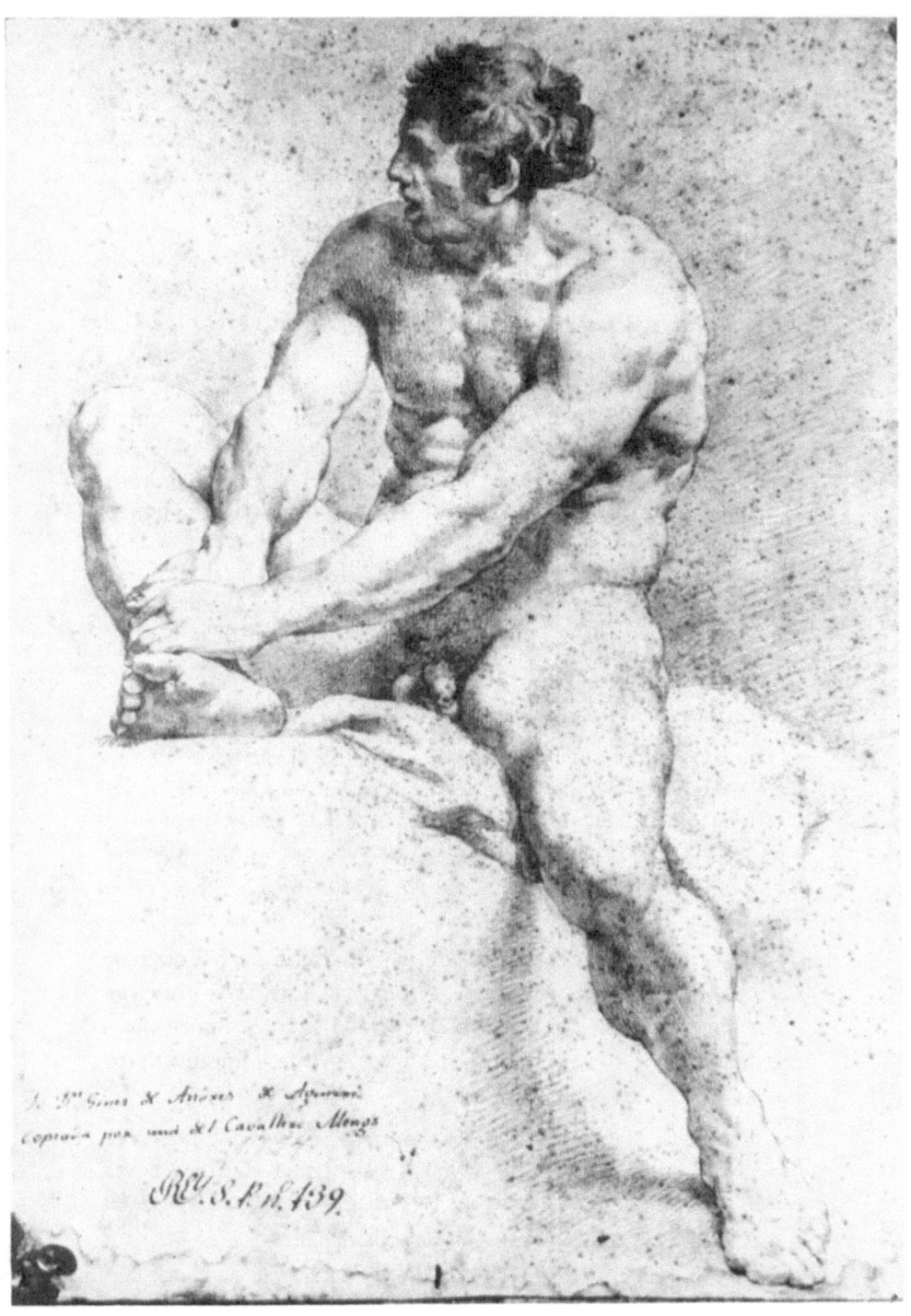

FIGURE 6. Ginés de Andrés y de Aguirre: Academy drawing, after a life drawing by Raphael Mengs. Charcoal on paper. Dated 1794. (Photograph by Lola Alvarez Bravo.)

Madrid Academy, Don Antonio Pons. Wrote Ginés de Andrés y de Aguirre:

. . . because of some fantastical promises in which I held much faith, I did not take time to ask for your advice or even to see you. I understand today what a mistake this was, for everything has come out the reverse of what was promised. Tired of spending, lacking success, lacking esteem—even before our arrival the seed of distrust had been sown. . . . Gil's only purpose has been to doggedly impose his opinions, forcing us to be present morning and afternoon, not excusing us at night, either, which is against His Majesty's commands in the Statutes. As a result, this foundation is brimming with abuses, either because the Board is ill-informed, or because its members believe Gil . . . and he keeps us from doing commissions for the public, and we must ask his permission to do anything, so that we deem our lot to be no better than that of prisoners.[15]

Don Cosme de Acuña y Troncoso wrote in part:

The condition I am in entails such bitterness that I would consider suicide were it not for the hope of succor . . . that is, to return to Spain come the New Year, in whatever condition that may be; for I hardly dare credit the common saying that he who fails to return a wealthy man from America is proved a mean head.[16]

This letter was entrusted for delivery to Don Fernando José Mangino, cofounder with Gil of the Academy. The message must have been sealed when Acuña gave it to his unsuspecting messenger, for it contains the following admonition to Pons:

Dn. Fernando Mangino has been the cornerstone of all the confusion and upsets that plague us now. I trust that you may never admit him into the Academy [of Madrid] . . . which would be

[15] Published *in toto* By Estrada, *Algunos papeles*, pp. 26–27.
[16] *Ibid.*, p. 27.

36

an occasion worthy of shedding tears of blood, even though he will advance the fact that he promoted this [Mexican] Academy; forgive my calling it by that name, for a more fitting appellation would be House of Confusion and Plots, or by another name, Gil's House.[17]

A third letter to Pons came from the director of architecture, Don Antonio Velázquez, who chimed in: "All is going like the devil, his [Gil's] only pursuit being to contribute to our total disgrace and to insure for himself the fame of oracle in all the arts."[18]

If the director of sculpture, Don José Arias, failed to add his voice to that of his colleagues, it was only because, after months of increasing strangeness in his actions, muttering to himself aloud and dragging furniture aimlessly around his room, he had at last lost his mind. At the time these letters were written, Arias was already confined in the Hospital de los Padres Belemitas de San Hipólito, where he died in December of that same year, 1788. Medical opinion gravely laid the mental disorder to "the rotting of some obstruction, a hardening, a lymphatical congestion or similar defect," which had "troubled the course and stream of his liquids and spirits toward the officious portion of the sensorial abode." Less learned and quite blunt was the opinion of Arias' colleagues, who unfailingly attributed his madness to "the outrages and the gall of one individual . . . primary source of all ills, the general director, Don Jerónimo Antonio Gil."[19]

While Arias escaped from Mexico only in death, the im-

[17] *Ibid.,* p. 28.   [18] *Ibid.,* p. 29.
[19] Carillo y Gariel, "Disputas y flaquezas que hacen historia," *Datos . . .,* pp. 46–48. I take the name of the hospital from Iñiguez, "La Academia de Bellas Artes." Carillo y Gariel calls it Hospital del Convento Betlemítico de San Francisco Javier. Both names may be correct.
Iñiguez (p. 36) quotes a diagnosis, dated August 25 and written by surgeon José Longino Martínez, which he accepts as a report of attempted

patient Acuña had to wait another decade before seeing his wish realized. In 1798, he was in Spain, having finally won the privilege of chaperoning a group of Mexican pensioners who had crossed the sea to round out their studies. The first offer of fellowships to Spain, made in 1793, had been met by a unanimous refusal from all six students selected, though under a variety of pretexts. José M. Guerrero and José M. Vásquez declined because they were married. Patiño and José M. López refused to travel under the supervision of Don Cosme de Acuña. José Gutiérrez and Joaquín Heredia feared the hazards of seafaring.[20]

In April, the King named Acuña, who had remained in Spain, one of his Court painters. In September, upon the death of its general director, Don Francisco Bayeu, the governing board of the Madrid Academy promoted to the post Bayeu's brother-in-law, the assistant director, Don Francisco Goya.

The modern approach to art history has been partial to

---

assassination: "La demencia que padece resultaba de varias pesadumbres entre ellas una poderossísima por sus circunstancias y efectos que inmediatamente experimentó [,] de haber tomado por fuerza una bebida enbenenada la que a poco tiempo bomitó." I would rather insert a comma between "experimentó" and "de," which gives the following reading: "His madness was brought about by a series of nightmares, one of which was especially vivid in its details and in its consequences, to wit, that he had been given by force a poisoned drink that he threw up soon after." This reading points to a case of paranoia more decided, but in harmony with the collective mood of the other members of the faculty.

[20] Revilla, *Obras,* note on pp. 5–6. A letter from Viceroy Revilla Gigedo to Don Antonio Porlier most likely comes close to the subconscious reason behind these refusals when it states that, though the advanced students doubtless should go to Spain to complete their studies, an obstacle would be that "owing to an exaggerated love of their Fatherland [Mexico] and its people, the natives prefer their own ways, even those who go about in the raw."—Arturo Arnáis y Freg, "Noticias sobre la Academia de Bellas Artes de San Carlos," *Anales del Instituto de Investigaciones Estéticas,* No. 2 (1938), p. 21.

whichever angles of Goya's life could be built up to show him a pre-romantic in style and a democrat in politics. As a result, today his name evokes for us cartoons and sketches rather than the formal compositions that were his bid for recognition. By the same token, it surprises us to observe with what ease and success the true Goya managed to live and move in academic and Court circles.

Contemporaneous appraisal was different from ours. When the Mexican Academy decided to acquire important paintings by masters to serve as academic models for its students, Mengs and Goya were listed side by side. Don Ramón de Posada—who was entrusted with the details of the negotiations—reported from Madrid on November 26, 1794:

With this in mind, and desirous also to meet Don Francisco Goya, I passed by his house. I found that he is totally deaf and that, if I were to converse with him, it would have to be in writing. In this fashion, I asked how ready was the picture that the Academy had commissioned from him and he answered that, because it was to have definite subject matter and nobody had appeared who could arrange a formal contract, he felt that he could not begin a work of such scope and fatigue while in doubt of the reward, and that, for the same reason, the other professors approached had also abstained.[21]

Acuña was invited in turn to fill the post vacated by Goya. As was his yearning, Acuña could now remain in Spain with honor, cleansed of the assumption that he was a "mean head."

Little of substance, either in works or in influences, remains of the passage through Mexico of this first phalanx of imported Academicians. It was reserved for the artists who came in the following decade as replacements to add permanently to Mexico's art patrimony, and to form disciples famed in their turn.

[21] Carillo y Gariel, *Datos . . .,* p. 28.

MEXICANIDAD AND THE ACADEMY

E VEN before Acuña left, another Spaniard was being sought for his department, "a teacher of painting possessed of the knowledge, ability, and dexterity needed to fulfill the obligations of Second Director of this noble art." The salary offered was 2,000 *pesos fuertes* ("sound money") per year, the position to go to the winner of a contest restricted to men who were already Academicians of Merit graduated from one of the two Royal academies, San Fernando of Madrid, or San Carlos of Valencia. Contestants were to register at the Madrid academy between January 20 and February 20, 1793. Within three

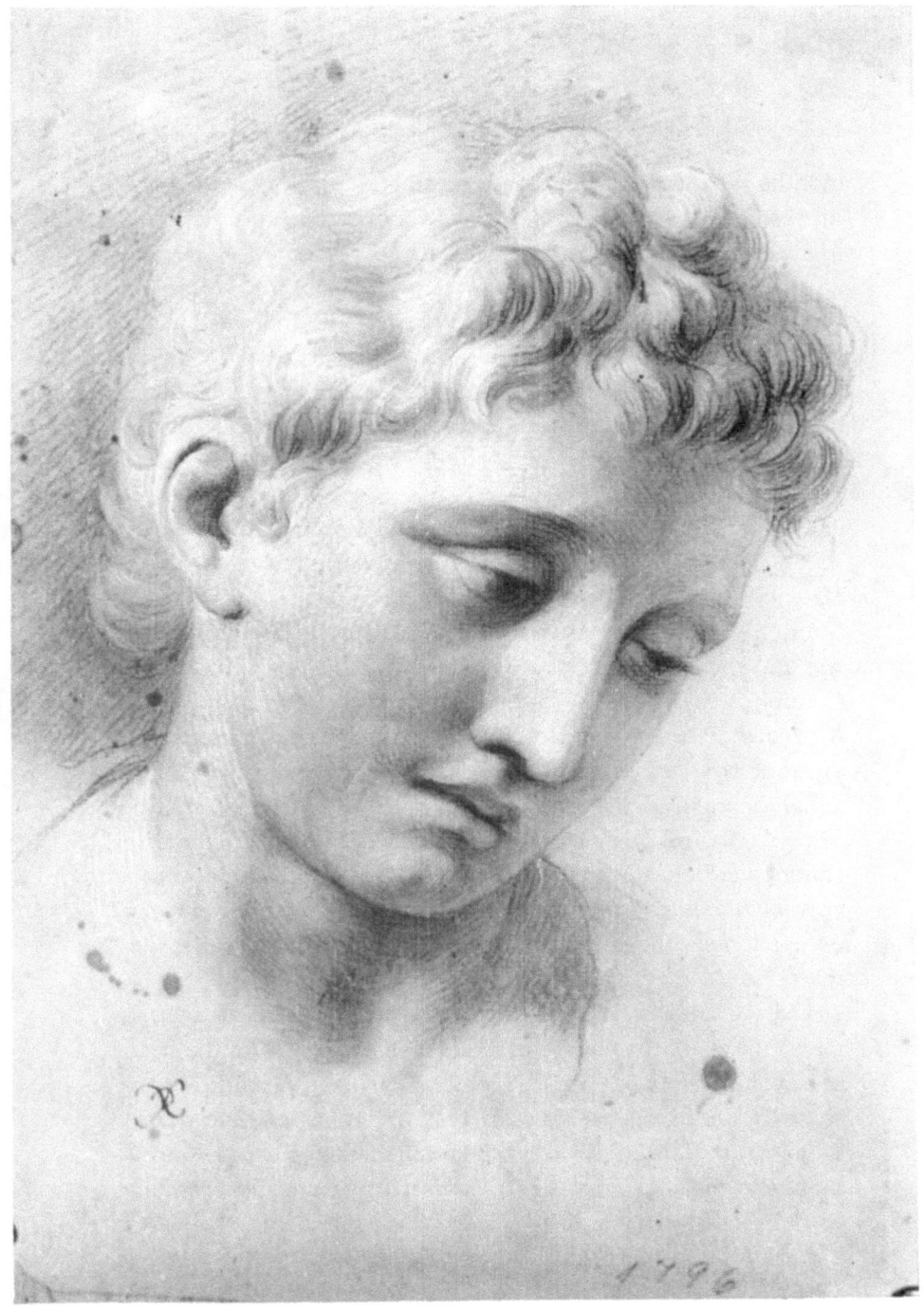

FIGURE 7. Rafael Ximeno y Planes: Head of a youth. Charcoal and chalk on tinted paper. Signed with his monogram, RXP. Dated 1796. (Photograph by Lola Alvarez Bravo.)

months each was to complete a painting on an assigned historical theme, after which, confined to a room of the school, he was
to execute a drawing in two hours, also on a designated theme,
and on paper marked in such a way as to make it impossible for
him to palm off a substitute. A first, second, and third place
were contemplated, the final results to be turned over to the
King to pick whichever candidate pleased him most, regardless
of placement. Only one candidate appeared, however, others
having been presumably put to flight by the disquieting rumors
that news from Mexico (such as those contained in the letters
quoted in the preceding chapter) could not fail to fan. The
solitary contestant, Don Rafael Ximeno y Planes, a native of
Valencia and a graduate of both Royal academies, went alone
through the involved proceedings. Aptly chosen by the judges
was the theme of his painting: "The Landing of Christopher
Columbus in America." A number of subjects were weighed
for the contest drawing, among them one Mexican theme: the
visits of courtesy exchanged between Captain Hernán Cortés
and Emperor Moctezuma. Less apposite was the final choice:
"The Archangel Raphael Guiding Tobias." However, "the professors were quite pleased with the drawing, which shows decisively the ableness of Ximeno to teach drawing, a principal
occupation of the directors of painting of the Royal Academies." [22]

Later studies by Ximeno, preserved at the Mexican school,
make one share the elation of his judges. Dated 1796, the head
of a youth (Fig. 7), in its blend of eighteenth-century non-
chalance and cool classicism, marks Ximeno as an able transi-
tional artist. The study of a naked man carrying a pole on his
shoulder (Fig. 8) is masterly in its perspective. Its very low
point of view with attendant distortions suggests it is a study for

[22] Estrada, "El nombramiento de Rafael Jimeno," *Algunos papeles,* pp.
39–48.

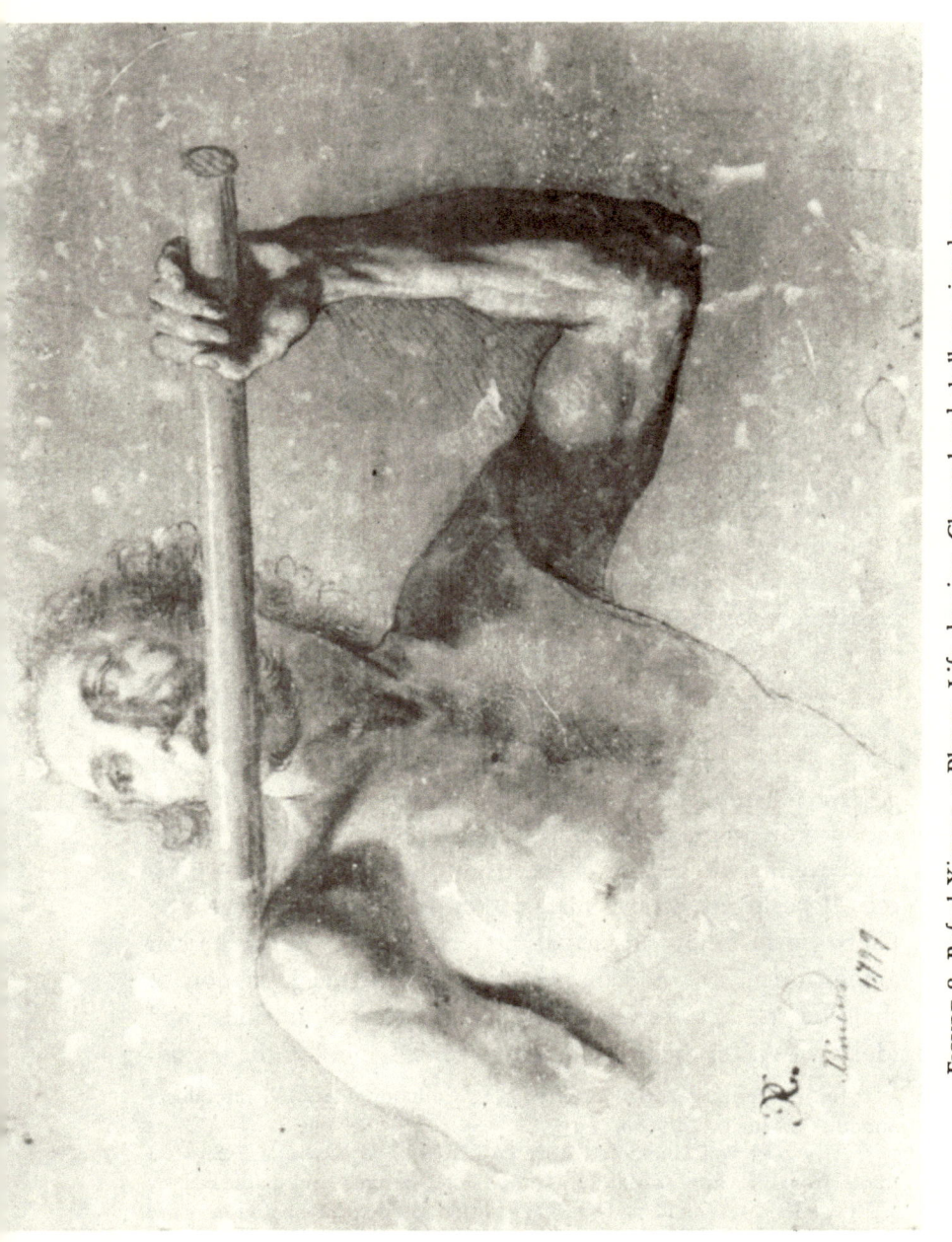

FIGURE 8. Rafael Ximeno y Planes: Life drawing. Charcoal and chalk on tinted paper. Signed with his monogram, RXP. Dated 1799. (Photograph by Lola Alvarez Bravo.)

some mural painting. Ximeno was indeed at his best when covering in tempera vast expanses of walls, as can still be appreciated in the single pendentive left in Santa Teresa (Fig. 9), the ceiling of the Chapel of the Palacio de Minería (Fig. 10), and the cupola of the Metropolitan Cathedral (Figs. 11, 12).[23]

Don Manuel Tolsá, named in 1790 to the direction of sculpture, brought with him from Spain the collection of plaster casts that Baron von Humboldt proclaimed superior to any he had seen in Germany.[24] Tolsá was talented both as an architect and as a sculptor, and at the death of Gil, in 1798, he became acting general director of the school. His masterpiece of architecture is probably the Palacio de Minería, sagging but still standing and used for a law school, with its complex vistas of staircases and colonnades. In the realm of sculpture, Tolsá's masterpiece is the monumental equestrian bronze representing Charles IV in the garb of a Roman emperor, which, for generations, has endeared itself to denizens of Mexico City under the affectionate nickname of *El Caballito* (The Little Horse).

The erection of the statue was originally meant as a political gesture, a flamboyant protestation of loyalty to the Crown from the viceroy, Marqués de Branciforte, who in 1795, in equally flamboyant style, begged of the King the approval of his project: "I positively believe that, if they [the Mexicans] were so happy as to enjoy the actual presence of the Regal Person among them, it would be necessary to curb the jubilation of their hearts, lest they fall into a paroxysm of madness and idolatry." As for the statue, it was to be "a symbol of the bound-

---

[23] Justino Fernández, *Arte Moderno, 2a.* Colloquy, Plate IX, reproduces another drawing by Ximeno.

[24] Alexander von Humboldt, *Essai Politique sur la Nouvelle Espagne.* I quote from the English edition (New York, printed and published by I. Riley, 1811), Vol. I, p. 159. This edition is cited hereinafter as *Essai Politique.*

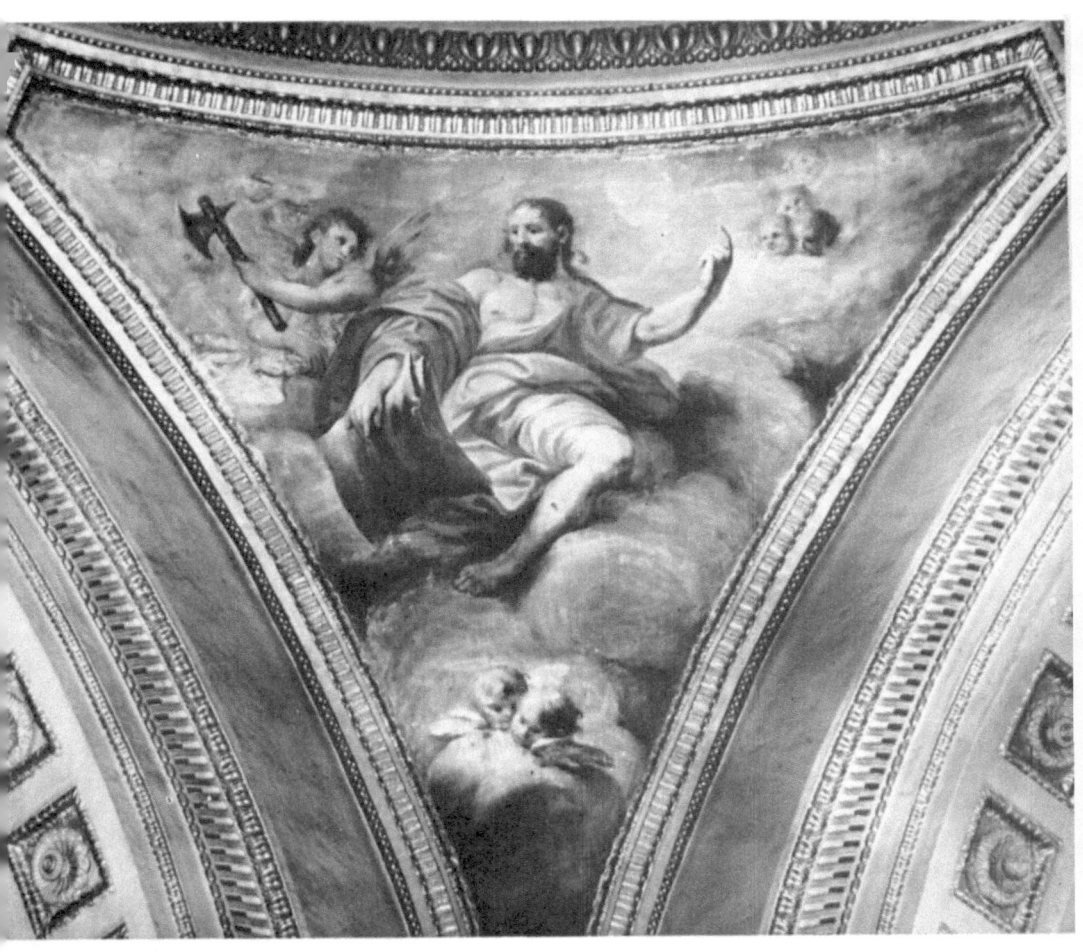

FIGURE 9. Rafael Ximeno y Planes: Saint Matthew. A pendentive in the Church of Santa Teresa, only remaining fragment of the decoration destroyed by an earthquake in 1845. Painted in 1813. (Gaud Foto.)

less serfdom pleasurably experienced by the docile, devout, and forever faithful Spanish Americans, who will remain so until the consummation of time."

From Tolsá's pen we have on the subject of *El Caballito* a workmanlike estimate of material expenses and a terse offer: "If Your Excellency plans to make use of my services in its execution . . . I am ready to do it for no other reward than that of pleasing Your Excellency, of serving His Majesty, and of being useful to the Nation." [25]

Bancroft has made it possible for us to dub in gestures and sound effects to the words of the Marqués de Branciforte: "When he took occasion to speak of the King, 'he melted, puckered his lips, sighed, and seemed transported into sweet delights, especially when he mentioned the benefactions of His [the King's] benign hands, and those of His Catholic bosom!' " [26] Though prone to poetical flights, the Marqués was practical enough where private gain was concerned. A suspicion

[25] Both citations from Federico Gómez de Orozco, "Documentos acerca de la estatua de Carlos IV," *Anales del Instituto de Investigaciones Estéticas*, No. 5, pp. 77–83. Fernández, *Arte Moderno, 2a* reproduces two drawings (Colloquy, Plate VIII, Figs. 28, 29) from the files of the Academy that he attributes to Tolsá. Both are after plaster casts and are indifferent in quality.

The authentic signature of a master on an Academy drawing does not always mean that he is the author of the drawing he endorses. Masters often signed student drawings as a mark of identification in closed-in contests, or when grading them. The problem of attribution is further complicated by the fact that drawings made by the masters served as models for those students who had not yet graduated to plaster casts, and most students' copies of that period came close to being facsimiles. Thus there exists in the Academy files a number of replicas of the sheet representing a man seated, seen from the back, originally drawn by Gil (see note 5). The safest guide for attribution remains quality.

[26] Hubert Howe Bancroft, *The Complete Works of Hubert Howe Bancroft*, Vol. XI (Vol. III of *History of Mexico, 1600–1803*) (San Francisco, A. L. Bancroft, 1883), p. 487 n. 8.

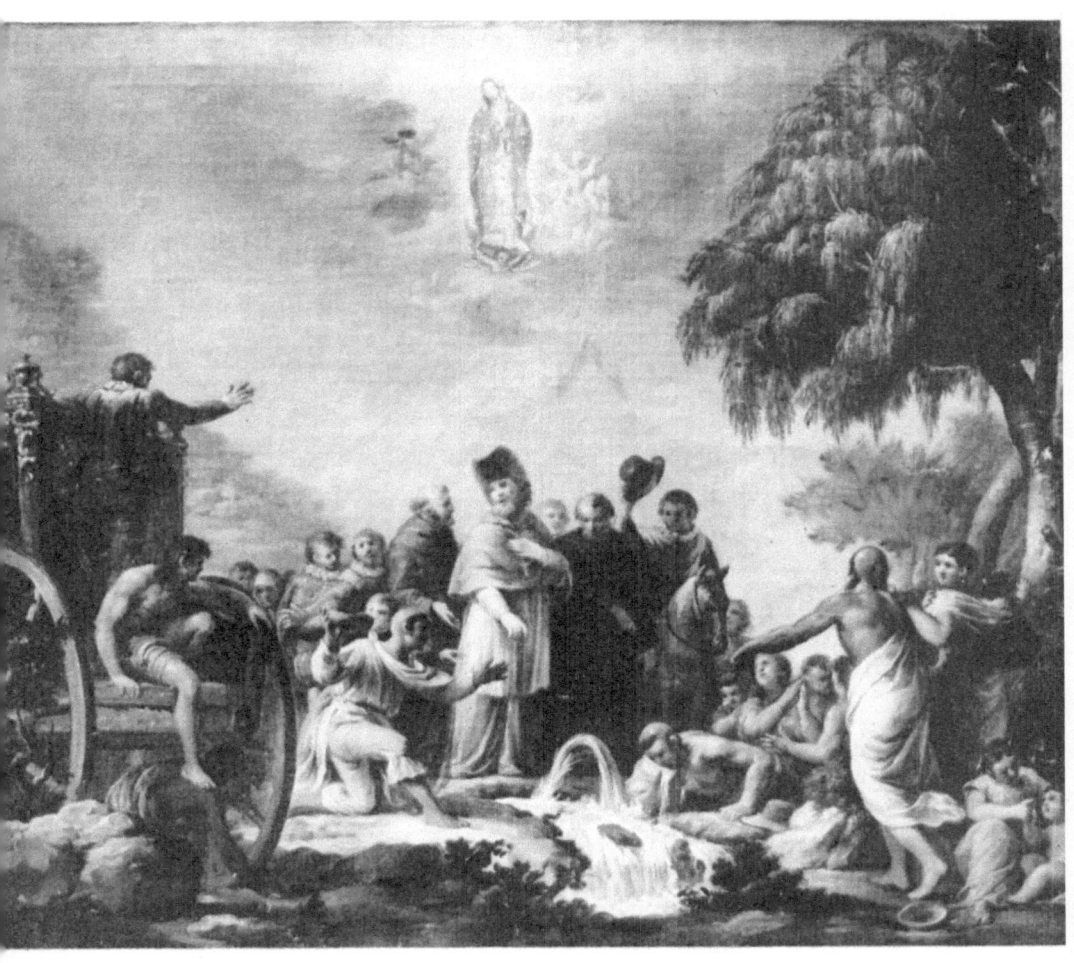

FIGURE 10. Rafael Ximeno y Planes: "The Miracle of the Spring." Sketch for the mural in the Colegio de Minería, Mexico City. Galleries of the Academy. (Archives of Dirección de Monumentos Coloniales.)

lingers that he used his exalted position to evade custom duties on merchandise from Spain that he would sell in Mexico for an exorbitant profit. The fact is that the Marqués returned home a far richer man than he had come.[27]

However astute as a businessman, the Marqués de Branciforte was a poor seer, for only seven years after the completion of *El Caballito* (1803) came the first uprising of malcontents that lit up the civil war. Tolsá's fiercely Loyalist creed impelled him to put again his skill and time at the service of His Majesty, this time in less-than-esthetic pursuits.

To better hound the rebels in the mountain fastnesses where their guerrillas hid, Tolsá constructed, "regardless of fatigue, fifty cannons given by the Royal Tribunal of Mining, and, without pay, another sixteen bronze cannons, and twelve mortars with their corresponding carriages, and besides paid over 1,600 pesos from his own purse for two mortars with their carriages, 120 rounds for a howitzer, grenades, and small shot."[28] That the Royal troops followed the insurgents into their stony strongholds is specifically alluded to in a letter, written to the King by El Conde de Heras as spokesman for the Academy, and dated June 26, 1817:

We have observed him [Tolsá] constructing furnaces, making molds and casting cannons, cannon balls, and sundry weapons, suitable for transportation to the mountain ranges and other wilds in which this land abounds. Some of these he paid for on his own, and made a gift of them to the Government. Thus bolstered, it was possible to terrorize Your Majesty's enemies, and to contain within bounds the deadly torrent ready to spread all about us its devastation.[29]

[27] *Ibid.,* p. 490.
[28] "Méritos y servicios de D. Manuel Tolsá," *Anales del Instituto de Investigaciones Estéticas,* No. 12, p. 33.
[29] *Ibid.,* p. 42.

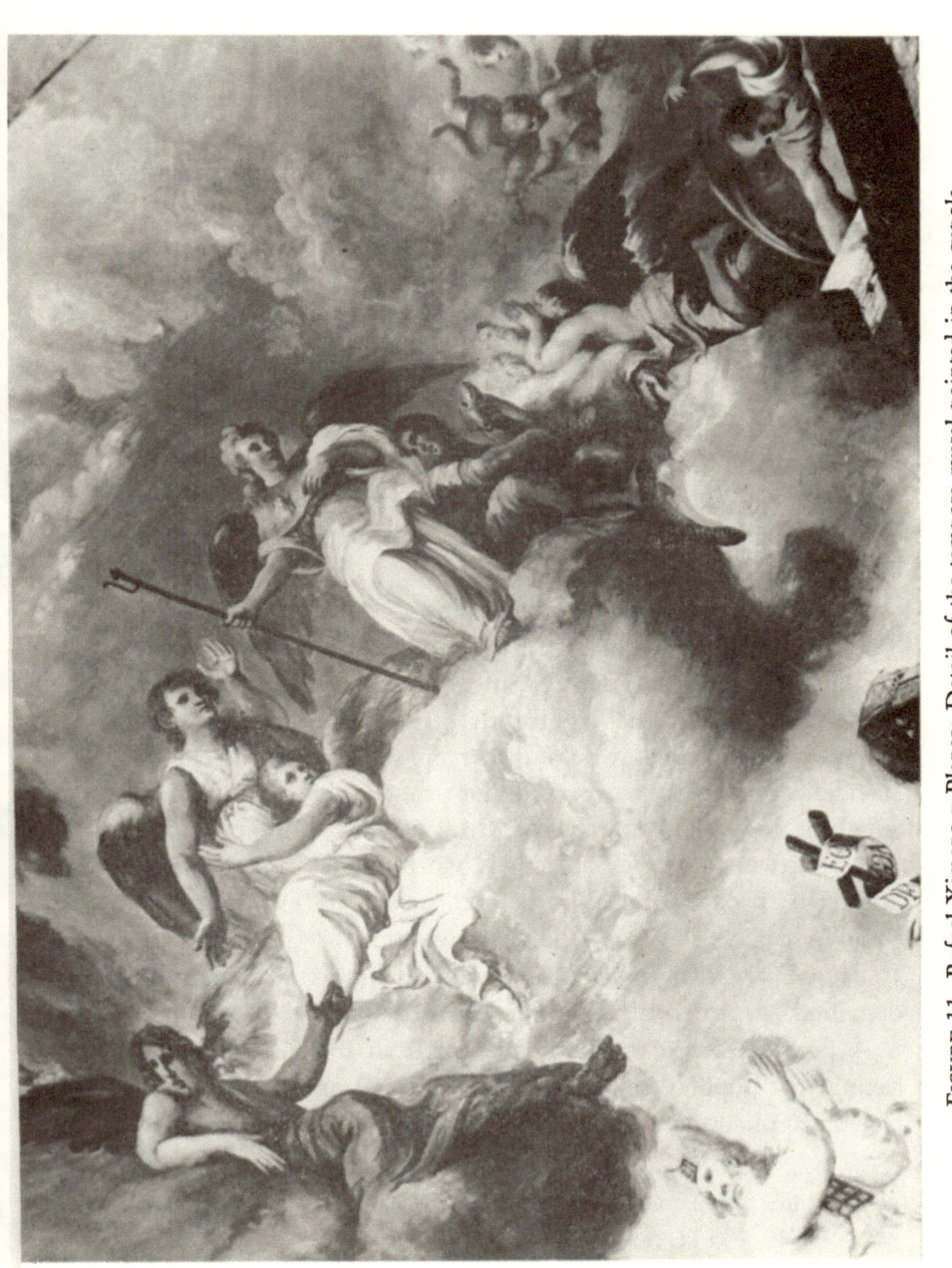

FIGURE 11. Rafael Ximeno y Planes: Detail of the tempera mural painted in the cupola of the Cathedral, Mexico City. Completed in 1810. (Archives of Dirección de Monumentos Coloniales.)

So great was Tolsá's fervor for the martial task that he asked and received from Viceroy Don Francisco Xavier de Lizana —who was also his bishop—license to do smith work on Sunday! [30]

A current simplification, and distortion, of history has it that Mexican Colonial society lived according to a caste system in which the full-blooded Indian played a role close to that of an untouchable. Even if this were the private attitude of the many, it nevertheless ran counter to Crown policies. These policies favored rather a paternalistic evaluation of the native that opened for him regal shelters closed legally to the white man. In matters of crafts—and painting came under this heading— the Government saw to it that Indian practitioners received protection.

So encompassing was this paternalistic attitude that it overlapped, and overruled at times, the no less legitimate preoccupations of men desirous of raising the standards of Mexican art production. In the eighteenth century, Academicians in tune with their times would throw up their hands in chaste scandalization as they observed the products of folk art that filled the streets and churches of Mexico, as plentiful and naïve and bizarre then as they are now. "Horror is felt at the many abuses, born of ignorance, to be seen in effigies, ex-votos, and public chapels. Our own shame is wrought at the hands of Indians, Spaniards, and Negroes, who, lacking rules and fundamentals, aspire to the imitation of Holy subjects." [31]

A petition was accordingly presented to the Government, asking that popular painting shops be closed unless their proprietors applied for, and were found worthy of, an endorsement

[30] *Ibid.,* p. 33.

[31] Carillo y Gariel, "Los artistas académicos y los tratantes y sus obradores," *Datos . . .,* pp. 21–23.

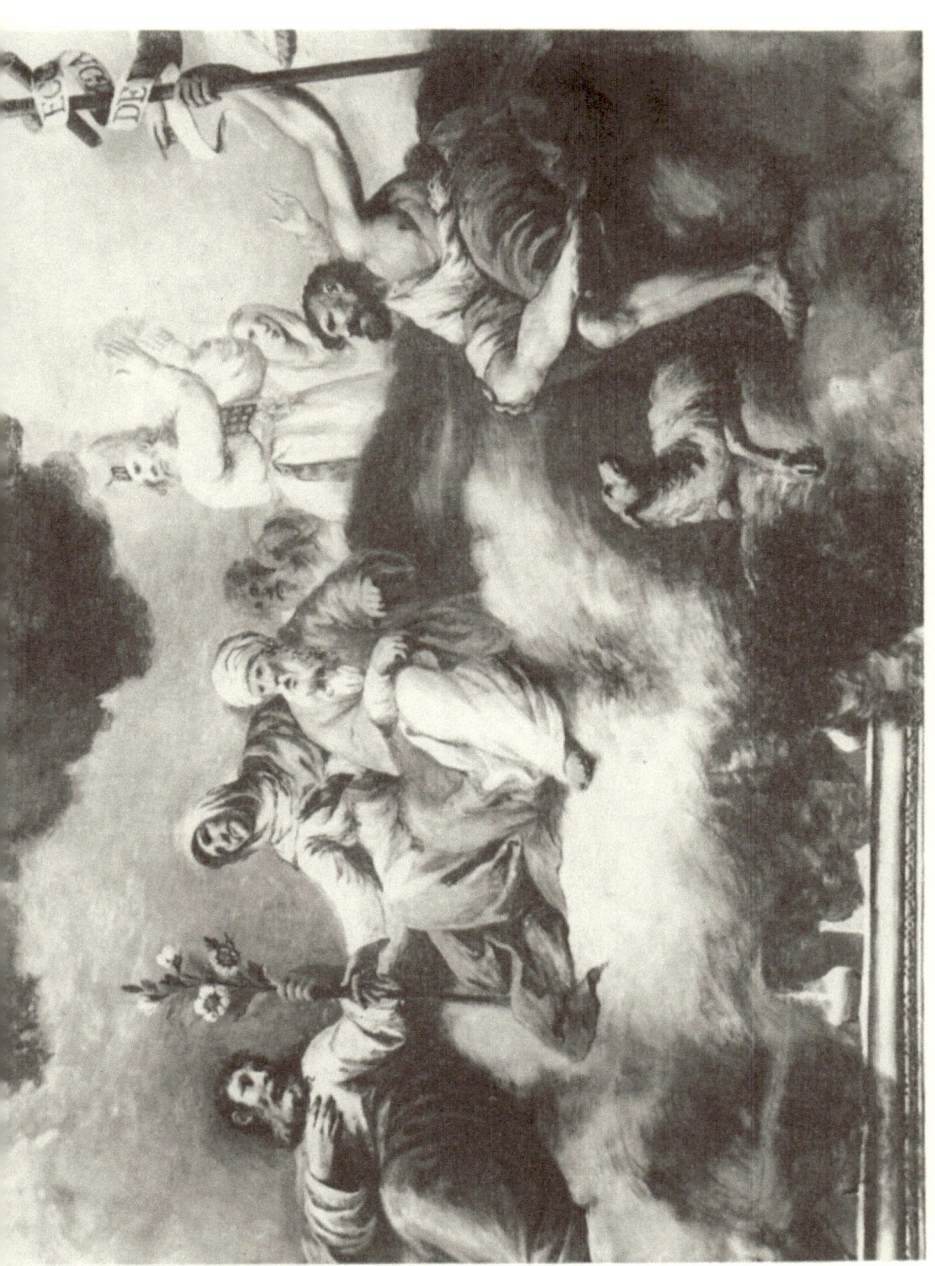

FIGURE 12. Rafael Ximeno y Planes: Detail of the tempera mural painted in the cupola of the Cathedral, Mexico City. Completed in 1810. (Archives of Dirrección de Monumentos Coloniales.)

by the Academy. In his answer, the fiscal approached refused to comply, taking instead a strong stand for the folk artists:

It would prove truly hard for so many poor fellows, Indians mostly, who have no other means of eking out a living than the little they make by executing paintings of a light nature. To deprive them of this occupation is to let them die for lack of an examination, or else force them to be examined when their exercise of the craft is confined to trifles, and when the poor fellows absolutely lack what it takes to finance the expense of an examination.

All the more striking is the fiscal's answer in that the Academicians had asked for no more than the enforcement of old guild statutes that had been decreed April 30, 1557, and confirmed October 7, 1686, whose efficacy had been allowed to lapse:

It is forbidden for any painter, maker of images, gilder, painter on panel or muralist, or painter on canvas to open a shop without first being examined by the inspectors of their craft, and to receive their approval. The fee for the examination shall be four gold pesos . . .

Said experts, at their own time, shall be empowered to visit the plazas, streets, shops, open-air shops and secondhand vendors, to discover any pictures not from the hand of a registered master, as the signature should show. They have authority to record the names of their authors, and to impound all pictures that fall short of art standards, or offend morally, and in order to enforce their decision may call on any agent at will.

According to these statutes, Indians were also required to take the examination but were exempted from paying for it—a fact that the fiscal seemed to ignore. As for those Indians who could not, or would not, pass the examination, "they are allowed to paint on panels flowers, fruits, animals, birds, decorative fantasies and such, thus avoiding the scandal attached to the bad rendering of Holy subjects." [32]

With hindsight, we may appreciate now how much folk art, art that we treasure by modern standards, was saved from extinction by this stand taken by a plain bureaucrat against the devotees of neo-classical canons.

The readiness of individuals to codify racial prejudice had come clearly to the fore when statutes were drafted in 1753 for the private academy of painter Miguel Cabrera. This short-lived venture that was based on racial discrimination failed also to receive official backing. Only with it might such harsh rulings as this one have been enforced:

None may receive students of mixed blood, and if anyone does so, inasmuch as it is against this statute, he shall be expelled when the Board hears of it. Furthermore, a professor, to receive students, must be a painter certified by this Academy. To abide by this ruling, the pedagogue must find out whether the child brought before him is a Spaniard and of good conduct . . . he will send him to the house of the Secretary . . . who will ascertain from the baptismal papers which the child brings with him whether he is of the quality he says; and if somebody wished perchance to be received who lacked these conditions, he should be advised that it cannot be done, as it is contrary to the Statutes . . . [33]

Three decades later, when the Royal Academy was founded, its rules, inspired by Crown policies, recorded a very different

[32] Francisco del Barrio Lorenzot, *Ordenanzas de Gremios de la Nueva España* . . . con introducción y al cuidado de Genaro Estrada (México, Dirección de Talleres Gráficos, 1921), pp. 19–23.

[33] "Estatutos o Constitutiones que deberá observar y guardar la Academia de la muy noble e inmemorial arte de la Pintura," Chap. 9. From a lost manuscript, quoted by José Bernardo Couto in *Diálogo,* p. 141, note 53. Couto saw—and apparently copied—the MS of these constitutions in the house of Don Francisco Abadiano, greatgrandson of Miguel Cabrera.

and unbiased approach to race; for example, as concerns awards
and pensions:

Essential qualifications of those eligible for these pensions are
that they be Spanish, born in those or these kingdoms, with the
precise and perpetual inclusion of four full-blooded Indians of
New Spain desirous to dedicate themselves to any one of the Arts
taught in this Institution, all having the union of poverty with
ability; so that, in the case that one be very poor, unless he also is
able, he shall not receive the pension; and even though he be very
able, if he is not very poor, he cannot receive it either.[34]

Underlining the ample-mindedness of this statute is the fact
that some of the pensioners went to study at the Academy of
San Fernando in Madrid, and that all could aspire to the degree
of *Académico de Mérito*—corresponding to that of Doctor of
Fine Arts in our own university system—plus honors that pres-
ent-day doctors are seldom accorded. Ruled the King:

To all Academicians of Merit who do not have letters of nobility
from other sources, I personally confer upon them all the immuni-
ties, prerogatives, and exemptions enjoyed by the nobles of my
Kingdoms; and I order that such privileges be observed and respected in any place where these men may settle, on the showing
of the pertinent document . . .[35]

That this ample-mindedness worked in practice is confirmed
by Baron von Humboldt, telling of his visit to the night classes
of the Academy in 1803:

In this assemblage . . . rank, colour, and race is confounded: we
see the Indian and the Mestizo sitting beside the white, and the son
of a poor artisan in emulation with the children of the great lords
of the country. It is a consolation to observe, that under every zone
the cultivation of science and art establishes a certain equality

[34] *Estatutos,* Statute 19, par. 2, p. 38.
[35] *Ibid.,* Statute 30, par. 5, p. 68.

54

among men, and obliterates for a time, at least, all those petty passions of which the effects are so prejudicial to social happiness.[36]

We can follow the seesaw of opinion that pitted private prejudice against Crown policy in the incidents attendant on the career of Pedro Patiño Ixtolinque—traditionally reputed a scion of Indian aristocracy—who became the first general director of the school to be nominated after Mexico had become a nation.

According to an act of baptism published, with reservations, by Carillo y Gariel as that of the artist, Patiño was born June 5, 1774, in the village of San Pedro Ecatzingo, of a Spanish father and Mestiza (mixed blood) mother.[37] Grown to be fourteen, the boy was living in Mexico City as one of the household of the assistant director of sculpture at the Academy, Don Santiago Cristóbal de Sandoval. In that year, 1788, Patiño applied for one of two pensions vacant at the time, but reserved for full-blooded Indians. Carillo y Gariel, to reconcile this move with the act of baptism, advances the theory that this was a false racial claim, a subterfuge prompted by economic need and contrived with the backing of the child's teacher, who was also his protector. However, pure Indians were alone exempted from some of the formalities, an exemption which proved a substantial advantage, and Patiño could hardly have applied as an Indian without exciting jealousy and gossip unless he was already known as an Indian by his teachers and fellow students.

The routine way to apply for a pension was as follows:

[36] Humboldt, *Essai Politique,* Vol. I, p. 161.

[37] Carillo y Gariel, *Datos . . .,* pp. 77–78. This act does not accord with the opinion of Patiño's contemporaries that he was a full-blooded Indian. By Mexican custom, a child from such blood as the act records would have been classified as white, especially as he is not referred to as *de color quebrado* (of mixed pigmentation). Further facts that I shall mention cast additional doubts on this document as referring to our Patiño.

Applicants shall present themselves to the Secretary, each with his act of baptism, and a memorandum covering the time that he has studied, together with a drawing or maquette from his hand, either a copy or invention, and with a certificate from the director . . . in charge of the classroom where he studies, stating that the work is from the hand of him who presents it.

As it sits in session, the Lower Board shall be shown the drawings or maquettes with the certificates, and shall vote on their merit. . . . This done, the higher Governing Board sitting in session shall be shown the memorandums: acts of baptism, and the votes of the Lower Board . . . also the recommendations of the teachers concerning ability and verification of poverty as investigated: I the King order that, prudently combining these two qualities—a point that I gravely charge to his conscience—each member vote for those he esteems most deserving . . .[38]

In the collection of the Academy there exists a Patiño drawing dated 1788, a crucial year for his career. The fact that it is preserved together with other prize drawings suggests it is the one that earned the young artist the fellowship. It is a carefully cross-hatched charcoal rendering after a plaster cast of the head of Apollo Belvedere (Fig. 13).[39] Baron von Humboldt men-

[38] *Estatutos,* Statute 19, pars. 3–5, pp. 38–39.

[39] The model was one of twelve plaster casts of different sizes included in the first lot of art works shipped from Spain as models for Gil's engraving school, about which there exists in the Spanish archives a correspondence from the year 1776 to 1778, published by Estrada, *Algunos papeles,* pp. 12–15.

Angulo Iñiguez tells how, of this first shipment, only four or five heads were found intact on unpacking, the rest being damaged.—"La Academia de Bellas Artes," p. 20. And Viceroy Flórez wrote to Madrid on October 27, 1788, "I beg you to speed sending the plaster casts, in view of the fact that the few owned by the Academy have been copied so many times by the students."—*Ibid.,* p. 24. In answer to this and similar later pleas, the famed plaster casts that Tolsá brought, also for the Academy, left Spain on February 20, 1791. As a precaution learned from precedent, Tolsá also

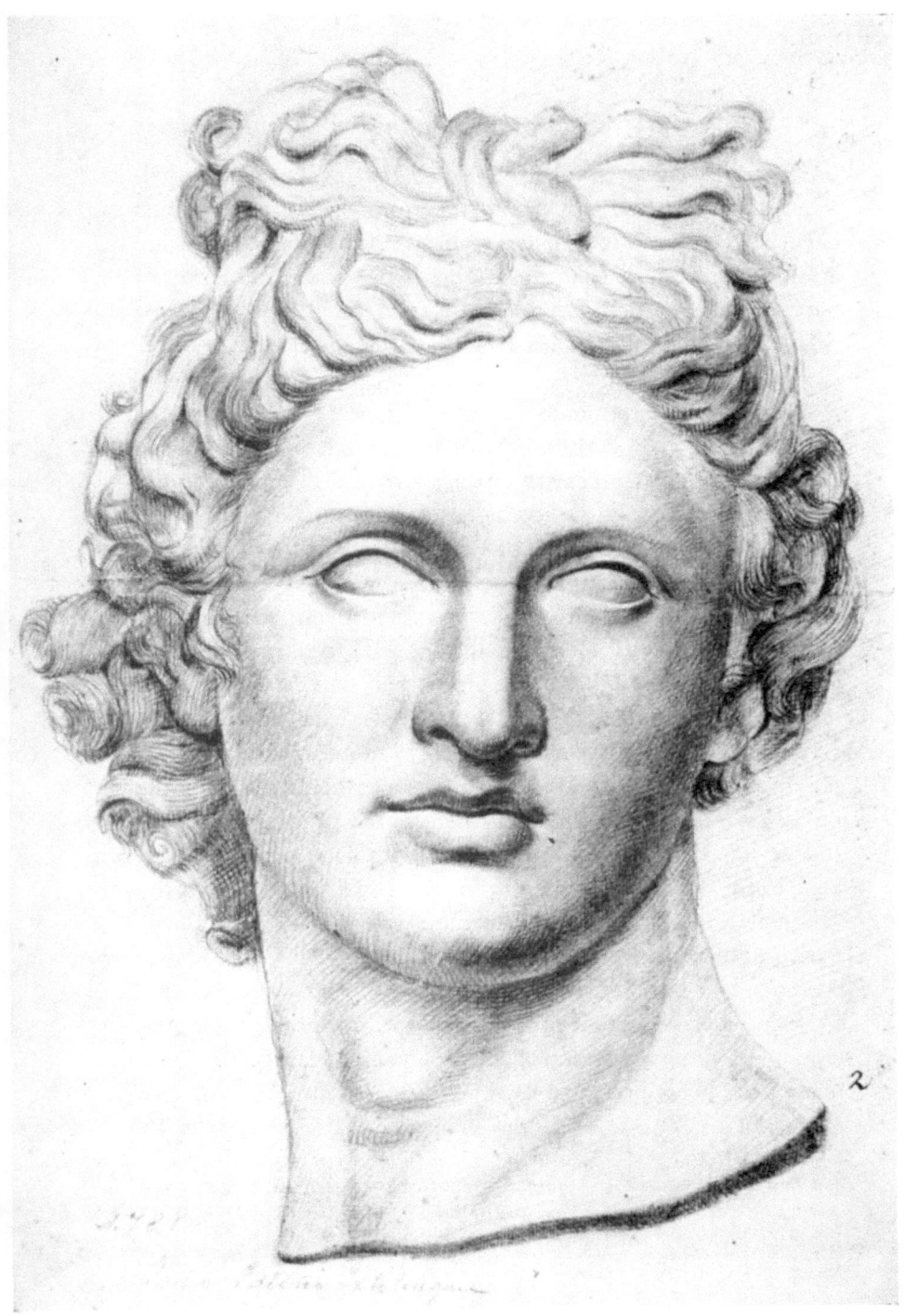

FIGURE 13. Pedro Patiño Ixtolinque: Drawing after a plaster cast of the head of the Apollo Belvedere. Dated 1788. (Photograph by Lola Alvarez Bravo.)

tions specifically an Apollo Belvedere that he saw in the galleries of the Academy in 1803, but, from the context, it must have been the full-length figure brought by Tolsá: "We are astonished on seeing that the Apollo of Belvedere, the group of Laocoön, and even more colossal statues have been conveyed through mountainous roads at least as narrow as those of St. Gothard . . ." [40]

Once accepted, the students received their pension for twelve years—"more than a sufficient time to acquire by unrelenting care the perfection necessary to their Art, and to make a living from its products," in the confident opinion of the King. [41]

Another drawing by student Patiño, dated 1796, falls within this twelve-year period. It illustrates his progress and the fact that he had graduated from plaster cast to live model. It transcribes an action "still," obviously contrived for anatomical display: "Burden-Bearer" (Fig. 14). When compared with the more polished exercises of fellow students, it shows the emergence of a personality somewhat awkward and somewhat brutal. In the weakness of a third dimension, noticeable in the respective positions of the feet, I believe that it also denotes an Indian hand. Such academic peccadilloes fade out, however, before a mood dramatic enough to make this drawing a worthy Colonial link between pre-Hispanic renderings of the "slave" theme and modern ones, fraught with social-conscious undercurrents.

Patiño was studying at that time under sculptor Tolsá, who employed him as assistant on many an important public commission. It is credible that Patiño's able Indian hand collaborated in Tolsá's great work, the equestrian statue of Charles IV

had sent with the casts 154 *quintales* (nearly a ton) of white gesso and stone for expected repairs.—*Ibid.*, p. 26.

[40] *Essai Politique,* Vol. I, p. 159.

[41] *Estatutos,* Statute 19, par. 6, p. 40.

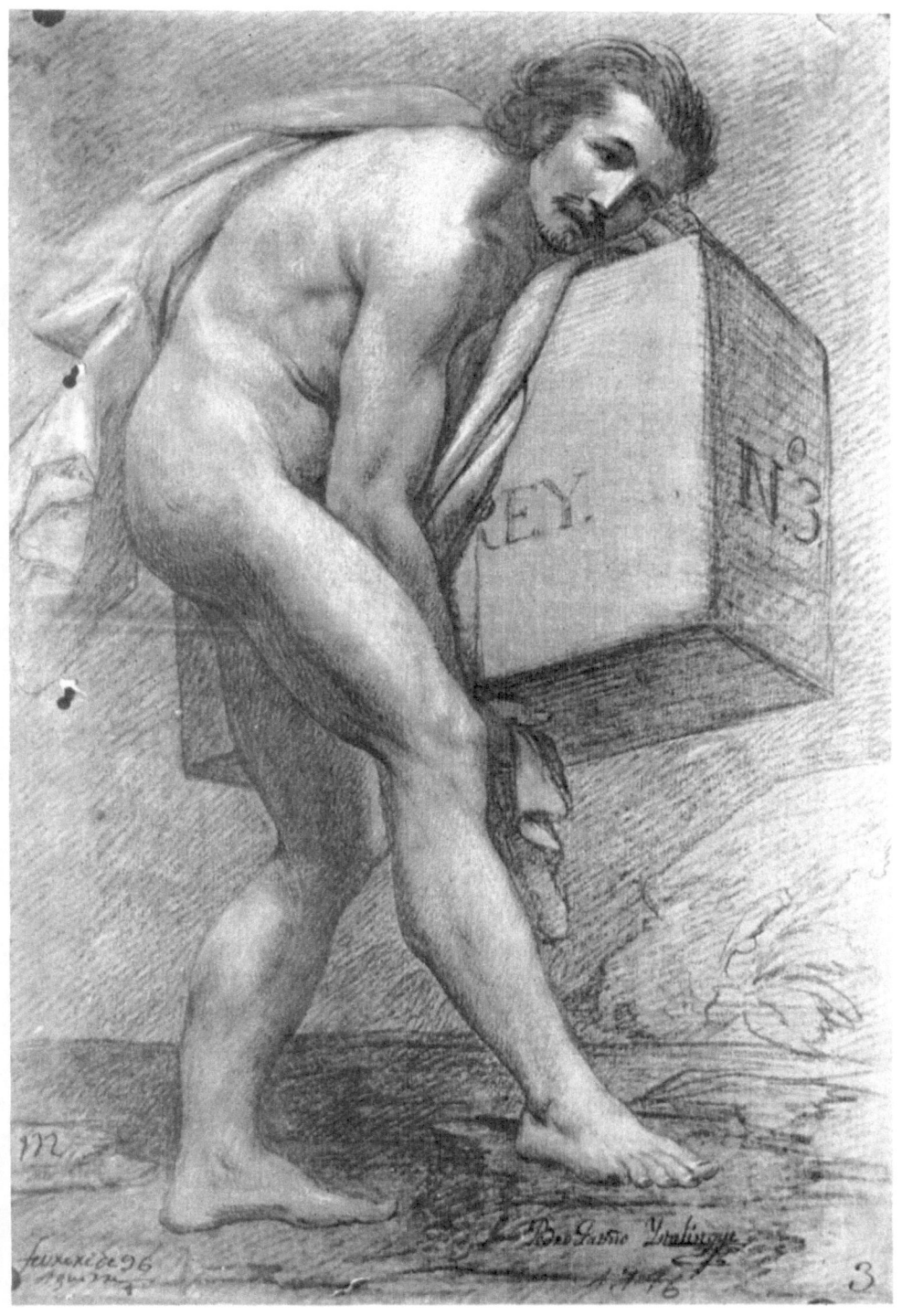

FIGURE 14. Pedro Patiño Ixtolinque: Life drawing, "Burden-Bearer."
Charcoal and chalk on tinted paper. Dated 1796. (Photograph by Lola
Alvarez Bravo.)

that shows the royal percheron trampling Indian weapons under its bronze bulk of 20,700 kilograms.

When Patiño's twelve-year pension expired in 1800, he remained at the Academy as assistant teacher of sculpture. A drawing, dated November, 1803, shows increased complexity and ability, especially in the rendering of depth (Fig. 15). An unusually Indian characteristic for the period is the drooping mouth and facial scowl of the seated figure.

Tolsá died in 1816 and was succeeded in the post of general director of the school by Ximeno y Planes. The following year Patiño applied for the coveted degree of *Académico de Mérito,* without which he could not have executed the official commissions to which he became heir:

If the aspirant is a painter he offers a picture on a historical theme; if a sculptor, a statue or bas-relief . . . Once the Vice-Protector or President has made sure that the work is truly made by the one who presents it, and having passed judgment privately . . . he offers the work to the judgment of the Board . . . admission or refusal to be decided by secret ballot . . . If the contestant is accepted as Academician, the work presented remains the property of the Academy.[42]

Patiño's offering was a bas-relief on the scholarly historical theme of Wamba the Goth being threatened with death by one of his electors as he refused the Royal Crown, which still exists in the collections of the school (Fig. 16).

Just as the Board was ready to sit in judgment, an incident occurred which delayed proceedings and which is recorded in full in the minutes of the meeting:

One of the trustees felt it his duty to state that, though Patiño, by his application and knowledge, deserved the degree to which he aspired, it was his opinion that Patiño's origin barred him from

---

[42] *Ibid.,* Statute 28, pars. 1–4, pp. 61–62.

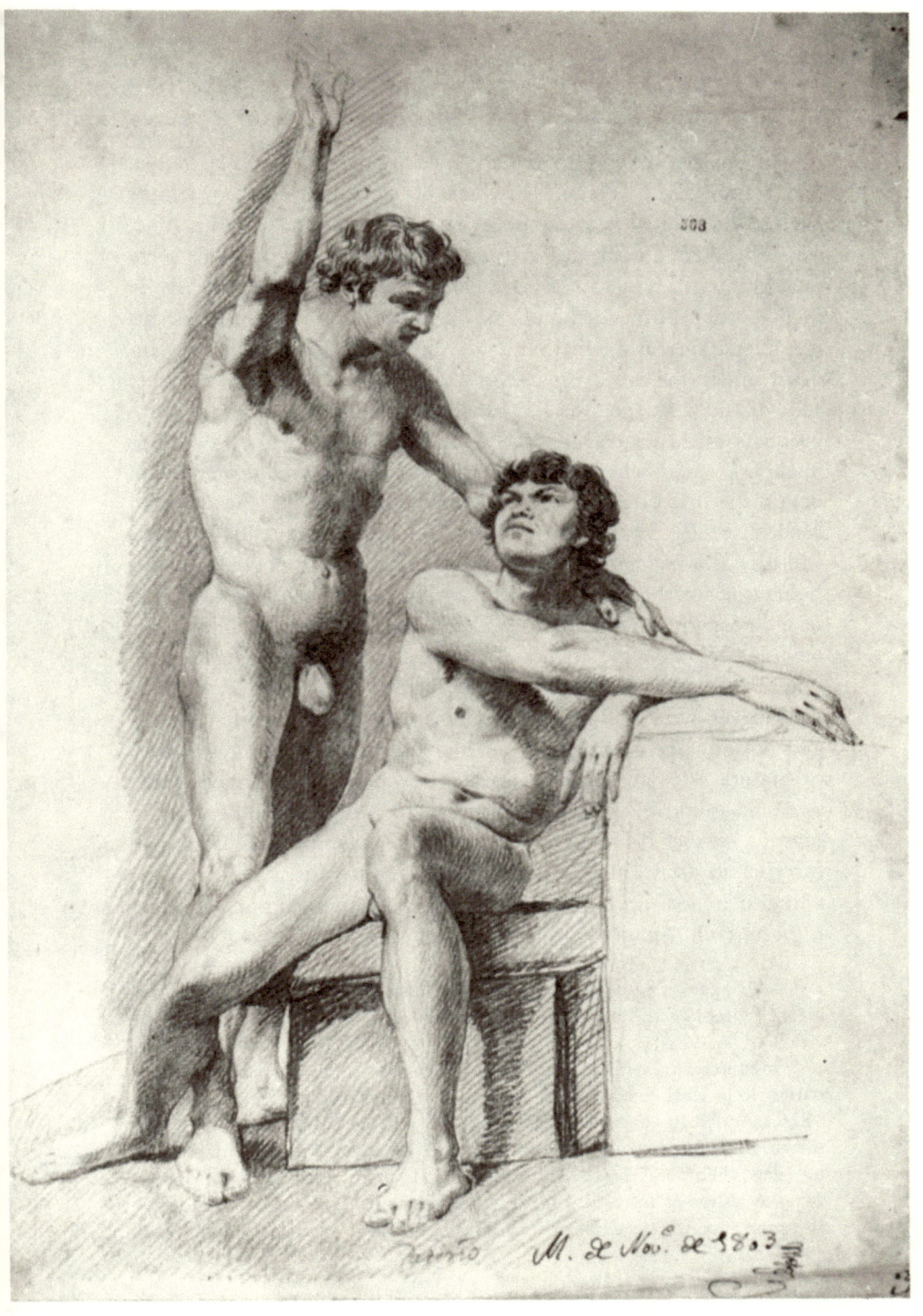

FIGURE 15. Pedro Patiño Ixtolinque: Life drawing. Charcoal on paper. Dated November, 1803. (Photograph by Lola Alvarez Bravo.)

competing, for he was an Indian, even though cacique and noble, and Statute 18, paragraph 9, which he caused to be read, admits exclusively Spaniards to the degree of Academician.[43] At this juncture, the point raised was discussed at length, and opinions were unanimous . . . as to the Sovereign benevolence being decisively in favor of full-blooded Indians, as is expressly manifest in Statute 19, paragraph 2, where His Majesty unequivocally includes Indians under the word *Spaniards,* making provision that precisely four of the pensioners be full-blooded Indians; that the same provision is made concerning the pensioners who are to be sent to Spain . . . and when telling of the hours and credits needed to obtain the title of *Académico de Mérito* of this Royal Academy of Madrid, tacitly declares all pensioners—and consequently also the full-blooded Indians—capable of obtaining said degree: if this holds true for the Royal Academy, with much more reason must it be true for this one. This, and other varied rules and solid reasons having been weighed circumspectly, all unanimously concluded— except the objector, who abstained from voting—that in no way whatsoever were full-blooded Indians excluded from the degrees and positions given by the Academy, and that the word *Spaniards* of Statute 18, paragraph 9, should be interpreted as having the same meaning as in Statute 19, paragraph 2, where the term is used as distinct from *foreigners,* its usual meaning in Europe and carrying its true Castilian significance, and not as a synonym for white men as distinct from Indians and dark-skinned ones, a meaning abusively acquired by the word in this America . . .[44]

[43] "All Spanish students, from this Kingdom as well as from the Indies, are fit to receive the posts of Academicians and other offices open at the Academy."—*Ibid.,* p. 37.

[44] Manuscript. In ink. "Libro de actas de las Juntas Generales y Ordinarias de la Real Academia de San Carlos Comenzado en Abl. del año de 1816." Added in pencil at a later writing, "a 18 de Julio de 1847." Under the title: "Recepción de D. Patiño Ixtolinque como Acad. de Mérito," at the date, February 4, 1817. Hereinafter I shall refer to this folio as Actas A. Another folio, also in the Archives, entitled "Actas y acuerdos de la Junta Superior de Gobierno. Comienza en 18 de Julio de 1848," with

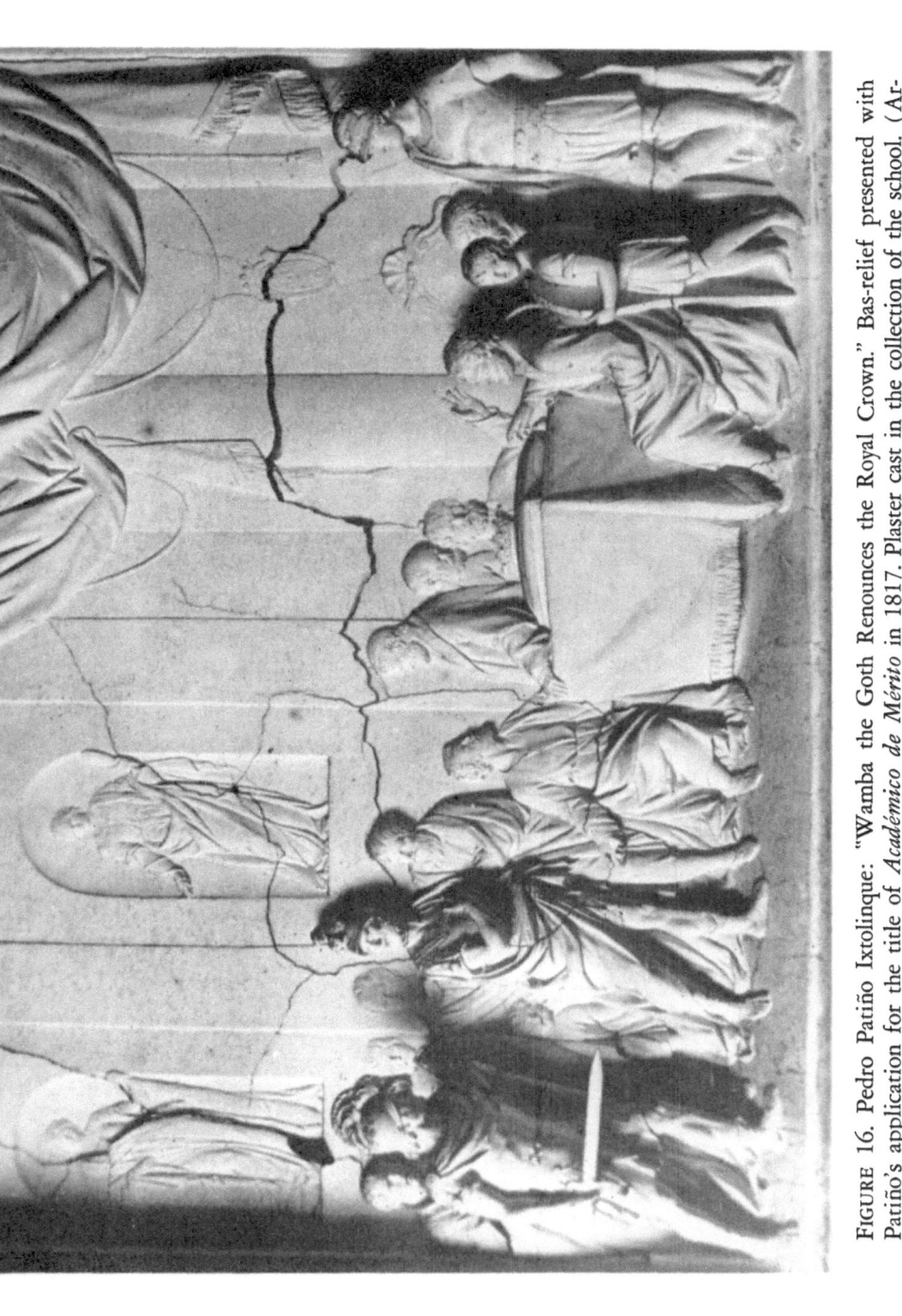

FIGURE 16. Pedro Patiño Ixtolinque: "Wamba the Goth Renounces the Royal Crown." Bas-relief presented with Patiño's application for the title of *Académico de Mérito* in 1817. Plaster cast in the collection of the school. (Archives of Dirección de Monumentos Coloniales.)

The discussion attendant upon the examination of Patiño makes it clear that all who consorted with the artist, both friend and foe, agreed that he was a full-blooded Indian, a logical inference being that his complexion and cast of features matched his racial claim. This unanimous agreement throws further doubt on the newly-advanced theory that Patiño was white, or at least of mixed blood, and on the pertinency of the baptismal act published by Carillo y Gariel as that of the artist.

A decorous academic knowledge is exuded by "Wamba," which shows but little of the strength of the freer drawings. Dull as it seems to us, it proved to be a matchless diplomatic performance that clinched Patiño's nomination.

The moment was one of chronic political and social unrest. Though the first rash of insurrection had been scotched, Colonial vested interests remained justly uneasy. Father Hidalgo, too, had appealed to race consciousness as he urged the Indians to rise on behalf of their ancestral rights and to dispossess the whites. Now that the whites found themselves again on top, if somewhat precariously, some saw it as their duty and salvation to solidly keep the Indian the underdog.

In those circumstances, the unnamed dissenter at Patiño's reception as Academician could feel justified on political grounds—and more so in retrospect as he considered the sequel. The racial slight first displayed in Tolsá's *El Caballito* had had time enough by now to emerge in Patiño's consciousness. Oblivious of his reciprocal duties to the Crown, the new Academician and aristocrat soon after his nomination took to the hills, there to join the republican insurgents, a lieutenant to the veteran guerrilla fighter General Vicente Guerrero.[45]

---

the later addition, "a Diciembre 27 de 1876," will be referred to as Actas B. Revilla, in *Obras* (pp. 12–14), makes extensive use of this report, but I believe that the actual text is here published for the first time.

[45] Revilla, *Obras,* p. 15. Revilla adds a probably apocryphal anecdote

As Patiño labored to achieve an independent Mexico, he sacrificed to the larger aim his care for the well-being of his school. Up to now its subsistence had depended upon donations received from the Crown, directly, or indirectly as the result of pressure exerted by the Sovereign on moneyed groups, the more substantial contributor being the silver-mining trust.[46] The independence that Patiño fought for was to make his school a pauper. For the period that follows, the registers of the Academy reflect the troubled times as each political upturn and each military coup jarred the school to its financial foundations. This drama of a crumbling outer world seeped casually into the reports of academic Board sessions, while faculty matters loomed large, such as the feud that smouldered over petty questions of precedence between the professor of mathematics and that of architecture.[47]

In 1820, the Colonial political structure was being axed not only from the left, but from the right as well. In Madrid, knuckling under the impact of a successful military coup, King

that is nevertheless of interest because it is of ancient origin and helped build posthumously the stature of Patiño as a confirmed insurgent. As it is told, when the revolutionary leader Morelos y Pavón was taken prisoner and shot in San Cristóbal Ecatepec, Patiño secretly took his death mask, already with an eye to erecting a future monument to this hero.

A death mask, traditionally called that of Morelos, does exist, and was deeded by the Patiño descendants to the nation, but its pedigree has been questioned. It is now believed to be a death mask of the artist himself. The anecdote, if true, would push back Patiño's insurgent leanings to before 1815.

[46] The original grants are published in *Estatutos*, pp. 4–5. As for the financial position in the early nineteenth century, according to Humboldt, "the revenues of the Academy of Fine Arts of Mexico amount to 125,000 francs, of which the government gives 60,000, the body of Mexican miners nearly 25,000, the *consulado*, or association of merchants of the capital, more than 1,500."—*Essai Politique,* Vol. I, p. 160.

[47] Actas A, February 11, 1820. "Pleito entre el Dr. de arquitectura y el de matemáticas."

Ferdinand swore to uphold a liberal constitution. In Mexico, regardless of his private conservative misgivings, Viceroy Don Juan Ruiz de Apodaca followed suit, setting June 17 as the day when all should affirm their adherence to the new order. With cautious alacrity, the Academy complied ahead of schedule, on June 15: "Today, in this Academy of the three Fine Arts of San Carlos in New Spain, was sworn the political constitution of the Spanish Monarchy"; [48] and in September, General Director Rafael Ximeno y Planes unveiled in Board session his portrait of the Viceroy, earning critical plaudits and a bonus of 50 pesos. [49]

As the liberal constitution became law, die-hards were heard to mutter discontentedly that the next step could only be an independent Mexico. One year later—September, 1821—their prediction came true when the National Army of the Three Guarantees made its gala entry into a delirious, beflagged, and beflowered capital. Its leader, General Iturbide, was named Regent to govern until the arrival of an as yet undesignated monarch who was to be eventually imported from Europe. With an alacrity equal to that shown in renewing its allegiance to the Crown, the Academy again anticipated the chosen day—October 27—when all were to swear allegiance to the new regime. Dropping from its name for the occasion obsolete references to its Colonial status and to its King, the Royal Academy was referred to at this time as the National Academy of the Three Fine Arts of San Carlos in Mexico.

For the bewildered members of the faculty, this meeting that was called "to swear allegiance to the Independence of the Mexican Empire" blended joy and sadness in equal parts:

October 26, 1821. . . . The President of the Board gave a short speech in which he rejoiced, as did everyone else, at the news of

[48] *Ibid.,* June 15, 1820.   [49] *Ibid.,* September 9, 1820.

the emancipation of the Empire; he described what unheard-of blessings were implied in such freedom; to all of which those present reacted joyfully.

Next, the Señor Presidente mentioned how employees had failed to receive their salaries, three months due, because of the national coffers—tobacco rent, City Fathers, association of merchants, and the mining trust—having suspended remittance of their monthly stipends. He suggested that a deputation be elected by the assembly to bring to the attention of the Most Excellent President of the Regency the plight of the institution.[50]

The President of the Regency, Don Agustín de Iturbide, was much too intent on plotting his coming metamorphosis into Emperor Agustín the First to devote practical thought to the quandaries of an art school, and the Academy was forced to close its doors before the end of the year. Travelers described the closed school:

We saw a long line of benches and desks, with designs and models for the pupils, as if they had left them yesterday, whereas no lessons have been given here for more than twelve months past.[51]

There is not a single pupil in the Academy; and though the venerable President [Ximeno y Planes] still lives, he is in a state of absolute indigence, and nearly blind.[52]

[50] *Ibid.,* October 26, 1821. A number of the more politically cautious members managed to avoid taking the oath: "The session opened with a report by the Secretary giving the reasons, either travel or illness, that made it impossible for some of the Academicians to be present."

[51] [Joel R. Poinsett], *Notes on Mexico, made in the autumn of 1822. Accompanied by an historical sketch of the revolution, and translations of official reports on the present state of the country.* With a map. By a citizen of the United States (Philadelphia, H. C. Carey and I. Lea, 1824), p. 72. Cited hereinafter as *Notes on Mexico.*

[52] W. Bullock, *Six months residence and travels in Mexico; containing remarks on the present state of New Spain, its natural productions, state of society, manufactures, trade, agriculture, antiquities, etc. By W. B.,* fellow of the Linnean, horticultural, geological and other societies . . . (Lon-

By February, 1824, Mexico had become a Republic and former Emperor Agustín the First an exile, soon to be under sentence of death. Owing to the unsettled state of the country a triumvirate of generals acted in lieu of a chief executive. Surprisingly, it was at last these military men who bent their collective ear to the protracted plight of the school, granting toward its rebirth 718 pesos monthly. Aging Director Ximeno y Planes "gave thanks to the members of the Governing Board for their zeal and application in resurrecting such a useful establishment." [53] Notwithstanding the gratitude the sum proved insufficient to alleviate even the most pressing difficulties. This state of affairs was aired on the following October after one of the triumvirate, General Guadalupe Victoria, had become First Magistrate. On this occasion the Board adopted a motion "to compliment the Most Excellent Señor Presidente of the United States of Mexico . . . who has offered to pay much care to the devising of succor and the compounding of remedies." [54]

---

don, John Murray, 1825), p. 160. Quotation is from the second edition. The trip made by Bullock lasted from March to August, 1823.

[53] Actas A, February 17, 1924.

[54] *Ibid.,* October 30, 1824.

FIRST STIRRINGS
OF A NATIONAL ART

THE period that opened in 1824—and stretches up to midcentury, when the famed reorganization of the school occurred—constitutes in its history the "dark ages." If scholars mention the Academy at all between 1824 and 1843, it is only to deplore what they term its collapse. It is true that economic rock-bottom was reached: gone were the Crown contributions of Colonial times, and yet to come the copious benefits that the school would derive from the funds of the National Lottery. Nevertheless, this wrongly-despised period is the only one before our time when faculty and students felt free to strive toward the elaboration of a national art. Before that, cultural directives were received, with Colonial orthodoxy, from the mother country. After that, as will be seen, esthetics were imported from Germany, via Rome and Barcelona, and still after that, from Paris.

Ximeno y Planes died in mid-1825, and his successor as general director was sculptor Patiño Ixtolinque. Patiño's worth as an artist, as well as his bold military record in the Revolution, surely entered into the choice. Moreover, the racial trend that had slowed his climb toward academic honors was now geared in reverse.

In Mexico there has always been a strong psychological bond between Indianism and nationalism. As early as 1565, in the halfhearted attempt at seceding from Spain known as the Avila-Cortés Conspiracy, the suspicions of the Loyalists were aroused at the sight of Spaniards masquerading as pre-Conquest Indians:

Alonso de Avila entered the City at the head of a fantastic cavalcade, consisting of twenty-four men richly clad as Indian lords and with masks in representation of diverse personages. Thus Avila appeared as Montezuma, and his attendants as members of the royal family and subordinate rulers . . ."[55]

In Colonial times, the symbolical graphic mottoes displayed in such things as vignettes, coats-of-arms, and funeral pyres picture Mexico as an Indian woman clad in pre-Hispanic vestments, paired with a Caucasian one, dressed in European costume, who symbolizes Spain.[56] Thus it was significant that in a

[55] Bancroft, Vol. II of *History of Mexico,* p. 610.

[56] Francisco de la Maza (*Las Tesis impresas de la antigua Universidad de México,* Estudio y selección . . . [México, Imprenta Universitaria, 1944]) reproduces two such figures (Plates 14, 15) that ornament a doctoral thesis of 1705. For nineteenth-century examples of Indianism, see Jean Charlot, "Juan Cordero, a Nineteenth-Century Mexican Muralist,"

Mexico where Indianism had always been linked with nationalism the choice of a director fell upon a full-blooded Indian once political independence was secured.

The initial spur to hero worship of leaders of the revolution was an official one, a first attempt by the Mexican government to use art for its propaganda value and for helping to cement national feeling:

On July 19, 1823, a law was enacted recognizing the services rendered in the first eleven years of the War of Independence as good and meritorious. Its promoters and leaders were declared "beneméritos de la patria en grado heroico," and their names were ordered to be inscribed in letters of gold in the hall of sessions of the national congress. Monuments to the memory of those who had suffered for the cause were ordered to be raised on the sites where they were executed . . .[57]

Patiño's nationalist stand was reflected more clearly in his choice of themes than in an evolution of his esthetics. Even as he worked on a monument honoring Revolutionary hero Morelos y Pavón, Patiño treasured the classical ideals of his Loyalist master Tolsá. Even when, as one of the details of this elaborate would-be mausoleum, he carved the figure of an Indian woman meant to symbolize America, it was along Greco-Roman lines —as the plumed masquerade of a weeping Niobe. And yet the craft of an Aztec hand is suggested by the directness of the carving, of a stockiness that bespeaks respect for his material— a local yellow stone quarried out of the Hacienda de la Calera.[58]

Art Bulletin, Vol. XXVIII, No. 4 (December, 1946), p. 251, note 17, last two paragraphs.

[57] Bancroft, Vol. V of *History of Mexico,* p. 9.

[58] Revilla, *Obras,* p. 18. The only other statue that Patiño executed for this never-to-be-completed monument represents "Liberty." At this writing, both figures, minus pedestals, flank the entrance to the main staircase of the San Carlos Academy.

Platiño's technique, unlike his esthetics, still showed some awareness of the pre-Hispanic tradition, of the unclassical—but true—worth of statues kept close to the original boulder shape.

In his teaching, Director Patiño departed more radically from neo-classicism than he dared do in his own creative work. The elaborate bust of a woman with flowers in her coiffure, dated 1827, was drawn by student Vicente Montiel and countersigned by Patiño as his teacher (Fig. 17). It shows that a picturesque Goyaesque influence was replacing the severe one of Mengs. Tame as they seem now, such mild attempts at *Mexicanismo* mark the first stirrings of a national art, concurrent with the birth of the nation itself.

Vicente Montiel became, in 1831, the first draftsman to be attached to the lithographic studio created by Patiño and directed by Ignacio Serrano.[59] Although lithography was an adjunct rather than an integral part of Academy curriculum, it seems fitting at this point to review its history in Mexico up to this time, even though doing so breaks somewhat into the narrative of events constituting the life of the Academy.

Lithography had been introduced into Mexico by Italian Claudio Linati, who was a bit of a Jacobin and a disciple of Jacques Louis David. In 1826 he opened his printing shop and began the publication of *El Iris,* a pocket-sized magazine illustrated with hand-colored lithographs.[60]

This innovation failed to be appreciated if we are to believe a letter from a reader to the newspaper *Aguila Mejicana:*

[59] Manuel Toussaint, *La Litografía en México* (México, Ediciones de la Biblioteca Nacional, 1934), p. 16. Cited hereinafter as *La Litografía.*

[60] *El Iris,* periódico crítico y literario, por Linati, Galli y Heredia. En la oficina del *Iris,* calle de S. Agustín núm. 13, y en las librerías de Recio, Ackerman y Valdés.

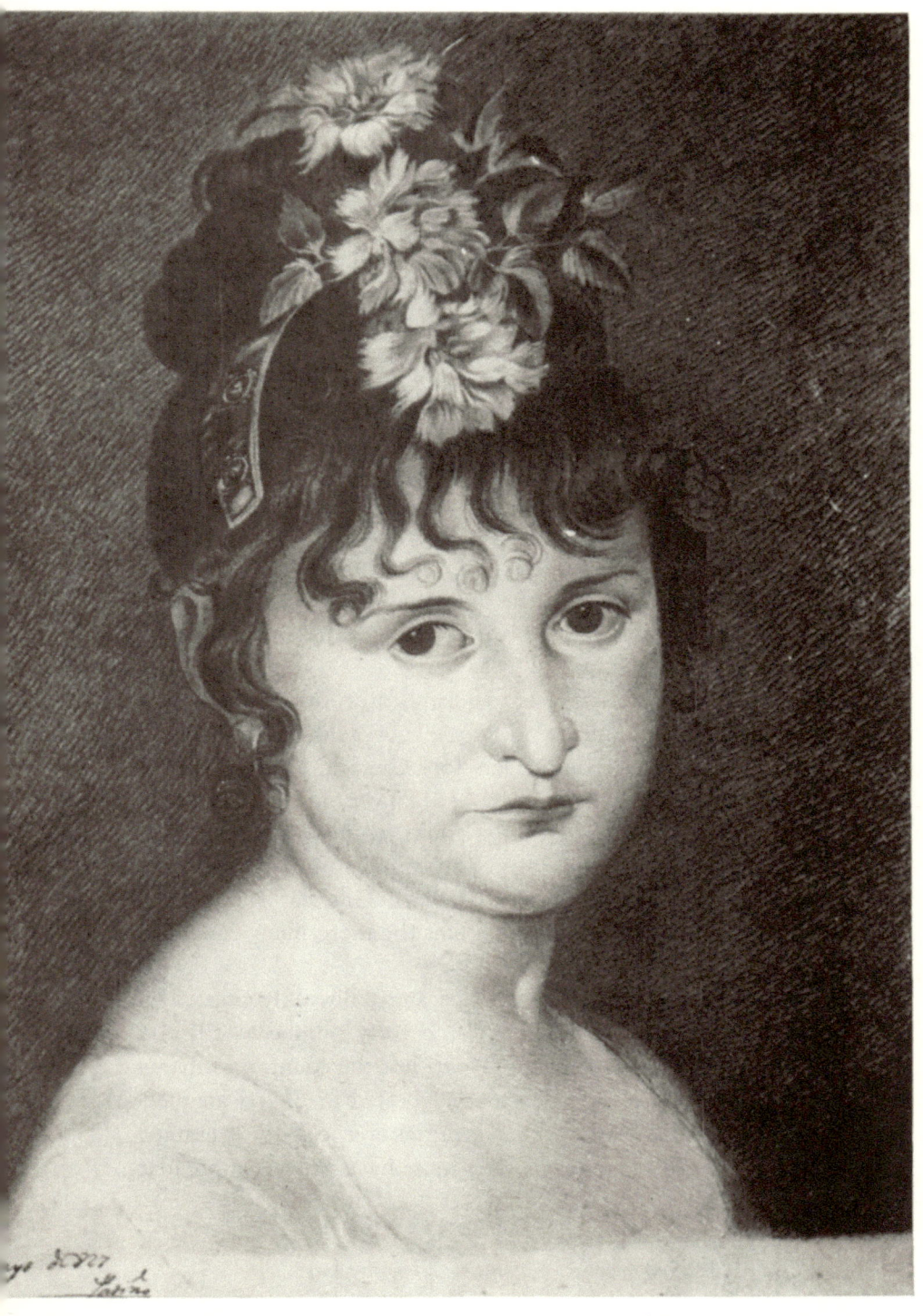

FIGURE 17. Vicente Montiel: Portrait drawing, countersigned by Patiño as his teacher. Dated May, 1827. (Photograph by Lola Alvarez Bravo.)

And something else I can predict is that *El Iris* will not last. To help keep it alive, may I suggest to its publishers that, from what I have heard, they would do well to omit the [fashion] plates and others, done in lithography, until they have mastered the technique. Maybe an exception could be made for the sheets of music, the one thing they have succeeded in printing not too badly up to now.[61]

Manuel Toussaint reproduces from *El Iris* a portrait of Hidalgo, bearing the tag "Litografiado por Linati."[62] Yet this is the one print in *El Iris* that we know to be by another hand; the portrait faces page 172, and on page 171 of the magazine a note states about "Hidalgo": "Concerning the lithographed portrait in this number of the magazine, it gives us pleasure to tell our subscribers that it is drawn and printed by a young Mexican."

Aguila Mejicana suggests two candidates for the authorship of this, the first published lithograph by a Mexican: "Intelligent and dedicated, young Don José Gracida, a native of Oaxaca, studied under Linati, and ended by printing better than his master. A [nother] cultured youth, a member of the General Staff, Señor Serrano, learned to engrave military and topographic maps in lithography."[63] Since Gracida is not mentioned as a draftsman, Serrano seems the more likely candidate for "Hidalgo."

El Iris began as a weekly, then became a biweekly. Started on February 4, 1826, it lasted through forty numbers—till August 2, 1826. That same year, Linati left the country, probably under political pressure. He had advocated in *El Iris* an independent general staff for the army as a check to attempted dictatorships, a suggestion which must have proved unpopular

[61] Vol. IV, No. 22 (May 22, 1826).
[62] *La Litografía,* Plate 1.
[63] July 9, 1826. Quoted in Toussaint, *La Litografía,* p. 13.

74

with the many would-be dictators. *Aguila Mejicana,* on May 22, 1826, threateningly advised the editors of *El Iris* that "when they refer to the Nation they should avoid belittling it, as happened in the opening lines of page 18, No. 16."

Linati's tie with Mexican art did not end with his departure. In Europe, he published a set of hand-illuminated lithographs, entitled *Costumes du Mexique,* that inaugurated the *costumbrista* series of graphic works that were to play an important role in the formation of a national pride.

In 1855, Joachín García Icazbalceta published a manuscript written by the pioneer draftsman and printer Don Hipólito Salazar on lithography in Mexico.[64] What Salazar tells of the period that preceded the establishment of the lithographic workshop at the Academy has been summed up in turn by Toussaint:

Don Ignacio Serrano supervised the lithographic engraving that Mariano Contreras executed: an allegorical drawing for an invitation to the festivities of September, 1830. It was printed in the studio of Don Pedro Patiño Ixtolinque, Director of Sculpture at the Academy. Another lithograph from the same source represents "un árbol de la cera" [waxberry myrtle], illustrating a report on its cultivation.[65]

The lithograph "Arbol de la cera," originally drawn and printed, according to Salazar, in 1830, was reprinted from the original stone in *El Mosaico Mexicano.*[66] The dilapidated state of the stone, coupled with the caption "Litogo. en la Academia de Megico," seems to justify the complaints of the next acting director, Don Ignacio Sánchez de Tagle, about the quality of

[64] *Noticias de la ciudad de México* (Escalante y Cía), p. 375.

[65] *La Litografía,* p. 16.

[66] *Colección de amedidades curiosas e instructivas* (México, Impreso por Ignacio Cumplido, 1836), Vol. I, facing p. 193.

lithography in Mexico and the Academy's identification with it (see p. 83). This pioneer print was replaced by a woodcut copy in the less rare but larger format reimpression of *El Mosaico Mexicano*.[67]

Anales del Instituto de Investigaciones Estéticas[68] published the correspondence, beginning on August 4, 1827, between Patiño, Tagle, and Government channels that resulted in the transfer of Linati's abandoned presses and utensils to the Academy. Serrano was named head of the workshop over two other applicants, Fournier and Pedro Robert. Patiño describes Serrano as "an Academy student, quite dedicated, and already advanced in this craft [lithography] as is proved by prints I own, among the latest ones he has done."

That the Academy graphic workshop failed to achieve eminence under Serrano is implied in the fact that Hipólito Salazar[69] thought that it had disappeared before 1837, while a report by Tagle[70] shows that it was still lingering on in 1839. Wrote Salazar: "During this time, and until 1837, what lithographs were issued came out of the printing shop of Rocha and Fournier, the only one there was, as the Academy plant was not active anymore."

So much for early lithography in Mexico.

Patiño died in 1835. Through most of the pre-reorganization period the care of the school fell to its acting director, the president of the Governing Board, Don Ignacio Sánchez de Tagle, who was also director of the Nacional Monte de Piedad. Born in 1782, Tagle had been connected with the Academy since 1805, having been named by the King as one of its counselors.

[67] *Ibid.* (México, 1840), Vol. I, p. 136.
[68] No. 1 (1937), p. 55.
[69] Icazbalceta, *Noticias de la ciudad de México*.
[70] Archives, 1839.

In between 1805 and 1835 lay an imposing political career—deputy to the Madrid Congress, redactor and signer of the Declaration of Independence, vice-governor of the State of Mexico.

The metamorphosis which turned into heroes men hunted as outlaws only a short while before was in progress, and art provided a potent vehicle for patriotic propaganda. In the same year (1830) that Patiño was carving the memorial to Morelos y Pavón, Tagle, who was a poet, was writing ringing verses in praise of the twentieth anniversary of Hidalgo's uprising:

.   .   .   .

> El mexicano así, por tres centurias,
> Esclavo tributario del Ibero,
> Para él trabaja, sufre mil penurias:
>
> Pero en fin, en Dolores el acero
> Vibra, y disipa esclavitud, injurias,
> Y el bando de opresores altanero.

> (Thus for three centuries the Mexican,
> A slave paying tribute to the Spaniard,
> Works for him and suffers a thousand miseries.
>
> But finally, at Dolores, steel
> Is bared, ending slavery, slights,
> And disbanding the haughty oppressors.) [71]

The political evolution of Tagle had taken him a long way since the day when, as official poet for the presentation of Tolsá's statue "Charles IV," he delivered a rhymed oration in praise of "La Lealtad Americana." His more usual poetical vein, aloof and reticent, is exemplified by the title of one of his odes: "To the Moon, in an Era of Civic Strife."

Only topical verses such as these became known in Tagle's lifetime. After his death, his sons took it upon themselves to

---

[71] Literal translation, with no attempt at rhyme or meter.

collect and publish their father's scattered production in two volumes, typographically handsome, with a portrait frontispiece of Tagle—aquiline nose, romantic mane, and side whiskers—facing a title page with ornaments printed in black, blue, and bronze.[72]

Tagle's executive worries were many. In 1834, the Academy was already nineteen months in arrears in its teachers' salaries.[73] The strictest economy had to be practiced in the matter

[72] *Obras poéticas del Señor Don Francisco Manuel Sánchez de Tagle,* recogidas y ordenadas por su hijo Don Agustín quien las publica a nombre de todos sus hermanos (México, Tipografía de R. Rafael. Series No. 13, 1852). The poem on Hidalgo is found in Vol. II, pp. 250–251; that on the moon, on p. 73 of the same volume.

An intimate source of knowledge for Tagle's life is the foreword to the published poems, written by his friend, the poet J. J. Pesado. A detailed factual account is also found in *El Album Mexicano,* Periódico de Literatura, Artes y Bellas Letras (México, Ignacio Cumplido, 1849), Vol. I, p. 110. A lithographed portrait of Tagle shows him with sparse white hair, ghosts only of the earlier windswept curls, hunched, and with the expression of apathy that characterized his last years: "National shame hurried his death. From the beginnings of the American invasion, he anticipated its lamentable results and related ills. He fell into extreme melancholy, which grew as he saw his fears being realized, and Mexico City being occupied by invaders.

"In resisting an attack by two bandits in one of the city streets, he was wounded in the hand, which made his condition worse, culminating in his death on December 7, 1847."

[73] Revilla, *Obras,* p. 15. The names of the members of the staff, and also their salaries, theoretical as they were at that period, are recorded in Archives, Book 22, *Comprobantes de data, 1833, 1834, 1835:*

Dr. Francisco Sánchez de Tagle, 1500 annually and 200 more for office help.

To the Director of Mathematics D. Manuel Castro	800
To Assistant Director of Engraving on Metal D. Manuel Aráoz	500
To Acting Professor of Architecture D. Joaquín Heredia	600
To Assistant Professor of Architecture D. Manuel Delgado	400
To the Proctor D. Estanislao Nájera	800
To expert D. Estanislao Rincón in gratification	8
To four pensioners [?] 4 pesos each per day	

of unavoidable expenses for materials—lamps, charcoal sticks, paper, rags. A memorandum dated 1839, and written in Tagle's own hand, details the meager offerings of the school:

STUDIES

Drawing in daytime. It is reduced to four persons who come, though without guidance, and to whom Don Estanislao Rincón,[74] without coercion of any kind and because he was begged to do it, gives corrections every four or eight days.

Drawing at night. Divided in three classrooms, one in charge of Don Miguel Aráoz (Fig. 18),[75] another of Velasco [subdirector

---

To the two handymen and the porter 12 pesos each

As to school expenses, we find in the Archives a typical weekly budget:

22 to 28 of November, 1835.

For 12 pesos' worth of candles	12
For 100 charcoal sticks	3.4
For a ream of paper	4.4
For the washing of rags	.3
	20.1

Even for this minimum expense, the school depended at times on charity. In 1830, the President of the Board writes: "In a way, I help support this indispensable institution. Since March of last year, out of my pocket comes the amount of 60 or 70 pesos needed every month to pay the minimum expense for lights, models, charcoals, etc."—Carillo y Gariel, *Datos . . .,* p. 90.

[74] Rincón had been teaching at the Academy since 1829. Beginning in November, 1838, he took over the class of Velasco. His salary was upped in June, 1839, by an additional 15 pesos per month. Rincón also taught, gratis, in the workshop of sculpture. He was relieved of its care when formal classes were resumed in October, 1840, under Don Francisco Terrazas. Rincón died on June 21, 1841, and his post was filled by Juan Suárez y Navarro.

[75] Aráoz was dean of the painting faculty. He is listed among the first students of the Academy, and sent in 1796 two drawings to the Academy of San Fernando in Madrid that were exhibited with the work of the other Mexican students (Estrada, *Algunos papeles,* p. 68). His drawing (Fig. 18) from a plaster bust, dated 1800, is the only one preserved in the files

79

of the school in 1837],[76] the other—in the corridor—in the care of Rincón.

Classroom of Aráoz. Because of the unprepossessing appearance of this individual,[77] his various idiosyncrasies, and the opinion generally held that his knowledge is small, no more than twenty or twenty-five students attend his class. He is never seen at the Academy in daytime.

---

of the school. It is of indifferent quality. He engraved in 1809 the "Apotheosis of Ferdinand VII," reproduced in Don Luis González Obregón, *La Vida en México en 1810*, p. 83. In the 1830's he was sub-director of engraving, at a salary of 500 pesos.

Dean Aráoz expected always, and seldom got, the respect of the younger faculty members. In the files for around the year 1840 are his rabid notes, complaining of slights and reporting the shortcomings of fellow teachers, written in a tiny script that retains an eighteenth-century flavor, on the right half only of sheets folded vertically in two. The pride with which he displayed his drawings as models for all students to behold irritated his colleagues, and Tagle, who notes: "Most of the originals displayed in the classrooms are very bad in the opinion of connoisseurs, while other very good ones are stored in the library. Because the former are by Aráoz, they cannot be shelved without his resenting it" (Archives, 1839).

So trying became the sight of the Dean's art that, in 1841, a newly-appointed teacher, Juan Suárez y Navarro, offered to the Academy as a gift a set of graphic works specifically "for the purpose of displaying them in the corridor where I correct. In my opinion, some drawings that are there should be taken down because they are very badly drawn, and others are totally useless" (Archives, 1841).

In February, 1842, Aráoz applied for a leave of absence because of ill health. This seems to have ended his active connection with the school (Archives, 1842).

[76] Ignacio Velasco's name does not reappear after the changes made in the faculty in September, 1840.

[77] The same passage about Aráoz is commented upon by Carillo y Gariel thus: "Aráoz, que a penas puede ver, no quiere enseñar sino principios . . . ." (Aráoz, whose sight is failing, refuses to teach any but elementary classes . . . .) "No quiere enseñar sino principios" is mis-applied to Aráoz. It is he, on the contrary, who insisted on teaching advanced drawing exclusively, and jealously forbade Rincón to share in its teaching.

80

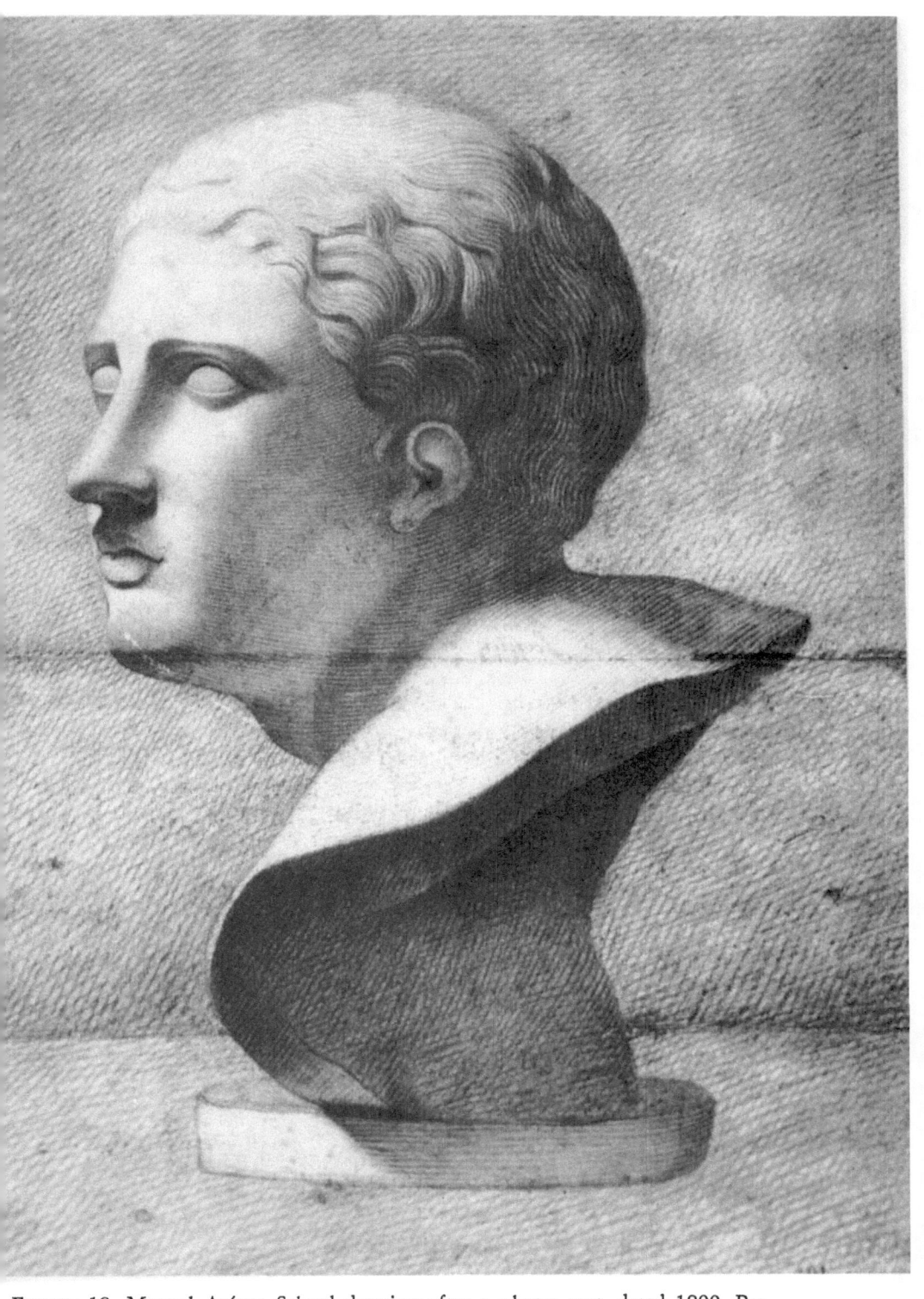

FIGURE 18. Manuel Aráoz: School drawing after a plaster cast, dated 1800. Perhaps one of those that he hung in the corridors of the school as a model for his students. (Photograph by Lola Alvarez Bravo)

Classroom of Velasco. Neither by day nor by night has he made act of presence for more than three years. At the end of March, he returned because he was prodded into doing it, but, soon after, he let it be known that he was sick and that Mata[78] should double for him. The latter answered that if he was made to double for Velasco he preferred to resign his pension and quit the Academy.

Corridor of Rincón. Thirty to forty students assist, and never does Rincón miss corrections, but because Aráoz sees to it that nothing is taught there but the first principles, as soon as they are qualified to pass to *manos,*[79] instead of entering the class-rooms, the students go away. . . .

Plaster cast. Once this classroom had to be closed because its students, and Mata also, had a fight with Aráoz concerning cor-

[78] Miguel Mata, born June 9, 1814, enrolled at the Academy in 1830. He received one of its first home fellowships, for which he did odd jobs and taught as assistant professor, becoming full professor in 1837, apparently without a corresponding raise. When Tagle asked Mata to take over the night classes of Velasco, who pleaded illness, Mata asked for an additional 25 pesos monthly, remarking that his pension was not of much help in practice: "Private lessons I give at night are paid twice the amount of my salary, and that salary exists only on paper at that, as not a cent of it has reached me" (Archives, 1837). In 1840, Mata went directly over Tagle's head to apply to the National Treasury for payment of three years' back pay, and with success. On October 30 of that year he was promoted to director of painting, with an annual salary of 350 pesos.

He was active in the initial steps toward the reorganization of the school: "The extreme poverty of the Academy proved to be Mata's chance to express his love for the school. He gave of his own money to keep it going. Also it was due to him that the sculpture galleries became a reality, as well as the restoration of the Academy itself and additions to it."—Francisco Sosa, *Biografías de Mexicanos Distinguidos,* Edición de la Secretaría de Fomento (México, Oficina Tipográfica de la Secretaría de Fomento, 1884), pp. 617–619.

[79] *Manos* refers to the study of extremities—casts of hands and feet—which followed the copying of drawings and engravings and preceded the study of plaster heads.

rections. When it reopened after three years, twelve came, mostly followers of Mata, and Mata himself. They would manage to have Mata correct them *sub rosa,* and now they are gone again because of the last correction that Aráoz gave, and only three students remain. . . .

Painting. It can be said that neither this branch nor that of *sculpture* exists in the Academy; what there is of it should rather be called public workshops set up on the premises of the establishment; the first is in the charge of Mata and the second of Rincón, but with no authorization whatsoever from the Academy; both are run by individuals impervious to inspection, inasmuch as they have not been assigned to these posts by the school; hence the school cannot be responsible for what errors occur there, or for the defective works to which birth is given; nevertheless, all this reflects discredit on the school. . . .

Architecture. An industrious mason was the only one who used to study, at night and without corrections. He fell ill and now nobody teaches and nobody studies.

Mathematics. Same as architecture. Different groups of boys alternately tried it; they became bored without an instructor and went away.

Lithography. It remains outside the inspection of the Academy, and the Serranos [80] are *de facto* its owners. They print circulars for the government and sundry works on which they make good profit. The stones are thinned so much by use that they disappear and the Academy is burdened with this responsibility and that of all that comes out of there, labeled as *done in the Academy,* be it good or bad, resulting again in discredit. . . .[81]

The year 1840 was climactic. In March or April, the Marquesa de Calderón de la Barca noted concerning her visit to the school:

[80] Ignacio and Diodoro Serrano.
[81] Tagle's report from Archives, 1839.

. . . the present disorder, the abandoned state of the building, the nonexistence of these excellent classes of sculpture and painting, and, above all, the low state of the fine arts in Mexico at the present day, are amongst the sad proofs, if any were wanting, of the melancholy effects produced by years of civil war and unsettled government. . . .[82]

Archives for that same year show that legal papers were served on the Academy in a litigation over 15,000 pesos of rent due.

The following letter from Vicente García to Sánchez de Tagle, president of the Board and acting director of the Academy, preceded the serving of the papers:

The rent owed to date for the building where the Academy of San Carlos is situated amounts to more than 15,000 pesos. As you are the one in charge, and as the money is so sacred a sum, considering the object for which it is earmarked, soon it shall be imperative to back my demand by legal resort.

When the Academy took over the premises in the eighteenth century, it dislodged the patients of the Hospital del Amor de Dios. Presumably the rent money endowed a similar charitable institution, El Hospital de San Andrés, whose governing board functioned as landlord to the Academy; hence the reference to "so sacred a sum, considering the object for which it is earmarked."

The Archives also show that the school debt to its faculty and employees equaled three years of their salaries. A note by Tagle, dated June 11, 1840, makes mention of the fact that when Mata received his back pay directly from the Treasury,

---

[82] Madame C—— de la B——, *Life in Mexico, During a Residence of Two Years in That Country,* with a preface by W. H. Prescott (London, Chapman and Hall, 1843), p. 103. The letter, dated April 3, is the thirteenth in the collection.

other employees "feel it is unfair that the payments [to Mata] were brought up to date, while theirs are three years in arrears."

Tagle apparently wrote an urgent plea to the Secretary of the Interior, stating that the school would have to close for a second time if it failed to obtain a monthly sum from the Government. At least, as much may be gathered from the following answer by the Secretary of the Interior to the unlocated letter of Tagle:

SECRETARY OF THE INTERIOR   *April 6, 1840*
I reported to the President what Your Excellency stated in your letter dated the third of this month: that if a monthly allowance sufficient to cover minimum expenses fails to be granted, the Academy of San Carlos will have to close its doors.

In September, in a try at reorganization, directors were named for the departments of painting, sculpture, and architecture: Miguel Mata for the department of painting, Don Francisco Terrazas for that of sculpture, and Don Joachín Heredia for that of architecture. Apprised of the fact, the President of the Republic, General Bustamante, proved how familiar he was with the acuteness of the situation:

His Excellency has ratified the nominations with the provision that the nominees should not fail to fulfill their obligations under the pretext of not being paid; in the end their salaries are to be paid in full for every one of the days that they show up in their respective classes.[83]

Thus for the debit side. If the Academy had been a business concern, the decadence on which critics dwell would be undeniable. But if our touchstone be not finances but esthetics, the period remains highly interesting because of willful and continued attempts to root its art into Mexican—or as contemporaries preferred to word it—into American soil. Already in

[83] Archives, 1840.

Colonial times, the term "American" was used as a badge of political noncomformism with Spanish rule on this continent. Wrote Humboldt:

The natives prefer the denomination of *Americans* to that of *Creoles*. Since the peace of Versailles, and, in particular, since the year 1789, we frequently hear proudly declared, 'I am not a Spaniard, I am an American!' words which betray the workings of a long resentment.[84]

After Independence, the proud connotation of the term "American" spread even to American subject matter in painting; for example, in the following passage, referring to Cordero's "Columbus": "How fitting it was to honor the memory of the famous Genoese from whom America received civilization, by the means of an American brush trained in Italy. . . . The powerful brush of Cordero was moved by an episode of concern to Americans, as well as by his gratitude to Italy."[85]

We owe a debt to Don Francisco Zarco for having clearly seen, and equally clearly recorded, what were the signs that, in midcentury, pointed toward the formation of a national style. In 1851, when he wrote the biographies both of Primitivo Miranda and of Juan Cordero, Zarco himself was only twenty-two years old and both painters were in their twenties. Had Zarco written later and in retrospect, he could not have captured as ably the enthusiasm for things Mexican that was as lucid as it was short-lived.

Even as we reread Tagle's report, from under the surface disorder of which he complained there emerges a more optimistic picture. Truly leavening was the role of Miguel Mata in the painting workshop, even though the Academy denied him its

[84] *Essai Politique,* Vol. I, p. 154.
[85] Francisco Zarco, "D. Juan Cordero," in *La Ilustración Mexicana* (1851), Vol. I, pp. 137–143.

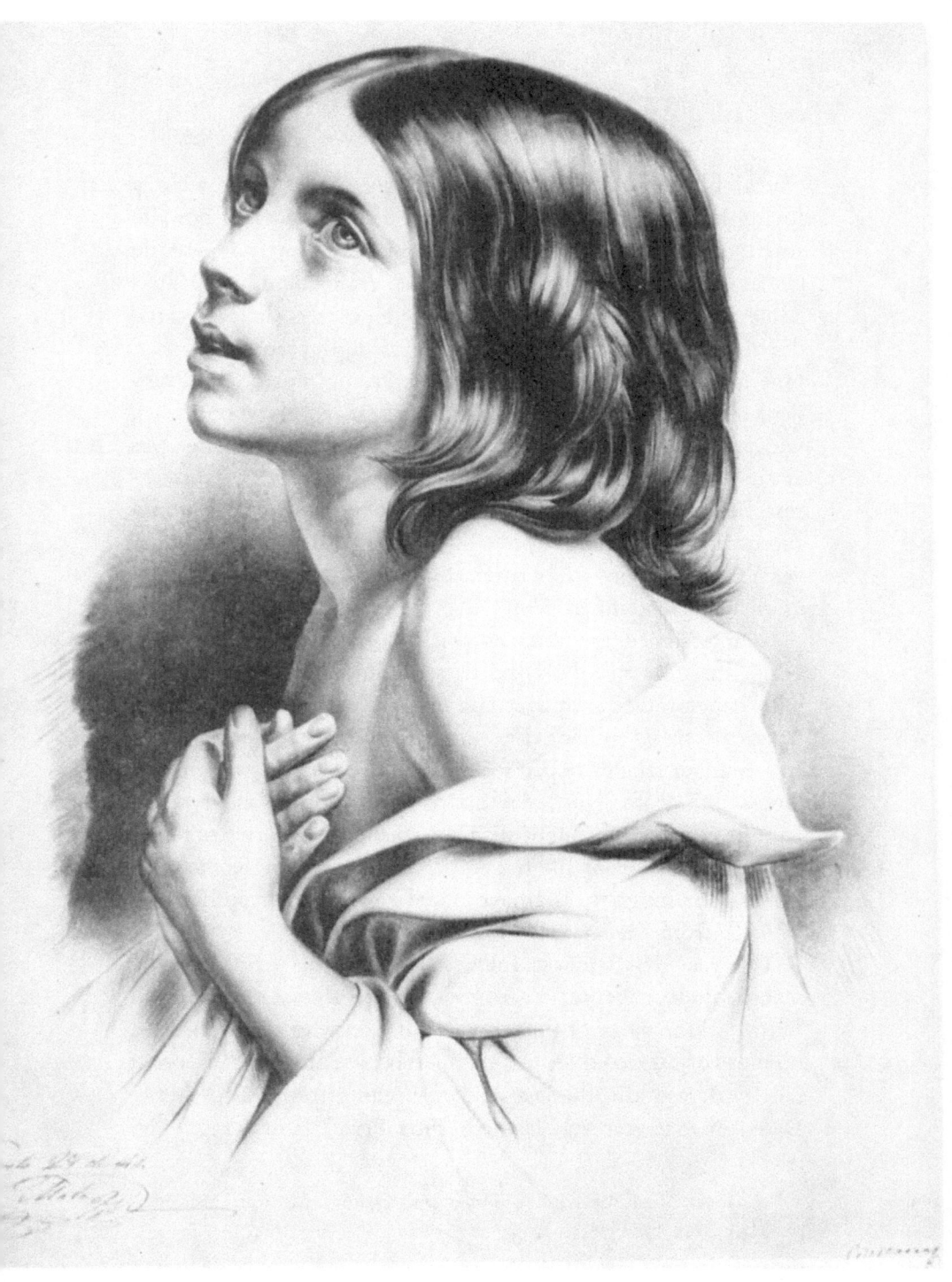

FIGURE 19. ——— Contreras: Drawing after a lithograph(?), counter-signed by Miguel Mata and dated August 28, 1844. (Photograph by Lola Alvarez Bravo.)

official blessing. The report unwittingly makes clear what a loving hold the young instructor had on the students; how he was the spearhead of a rebellion against the—by now—senile classical element personified by Manuel Aráoz; and how Mata's adolescent admirers would ask him to correct in secret the drawings they made under the official supervision of Aráoz. One is tempted to make slight of the grumblings of the President of the Board as he describes the sight of very young men, without compulsion or eventual credits, grouping themselves around their twenty-five-year-old teacher. Furthermore, this unrest, being a valid sign of the times, proved to be in the end a successful revolution. *De facto* director of painting in 1839, the year Tagle's report was written, Mata was recognized officially as such in September, 1840.

Countersigned by Mata as teacher, and dated August 28, 1844, the drawing of a child by student Contreras (Fig. 19), with hands folded in prayer and eyes raised heavenward, illustrates the suave romanticism with which young Mata and his still younger friends hoped to supplant the waning influence of Greek and Roman art. An impressive proof of the type of painting that Mata taught in his workshop is the portrait that Juan Cordero did of his father before leaving for Rome, also in 1844. It suggests, as I have noted elsewhere, an infiltration of style from the mature Goya.[86]

The year 1845 marks the last year of this period of the school's independence, for contracts were signed that year in Europe in the name of the school with men who comprehended no more of Mexico than had the members of that first imported faculty. It was also the last year of teaching freedom for Mata. Dated of that year and labeled "First Prize," a drawing (Fig.

[86] Charlot, "Juan Cordero, a Nineteenth-Century Mexican Muralist," p. 251.

88

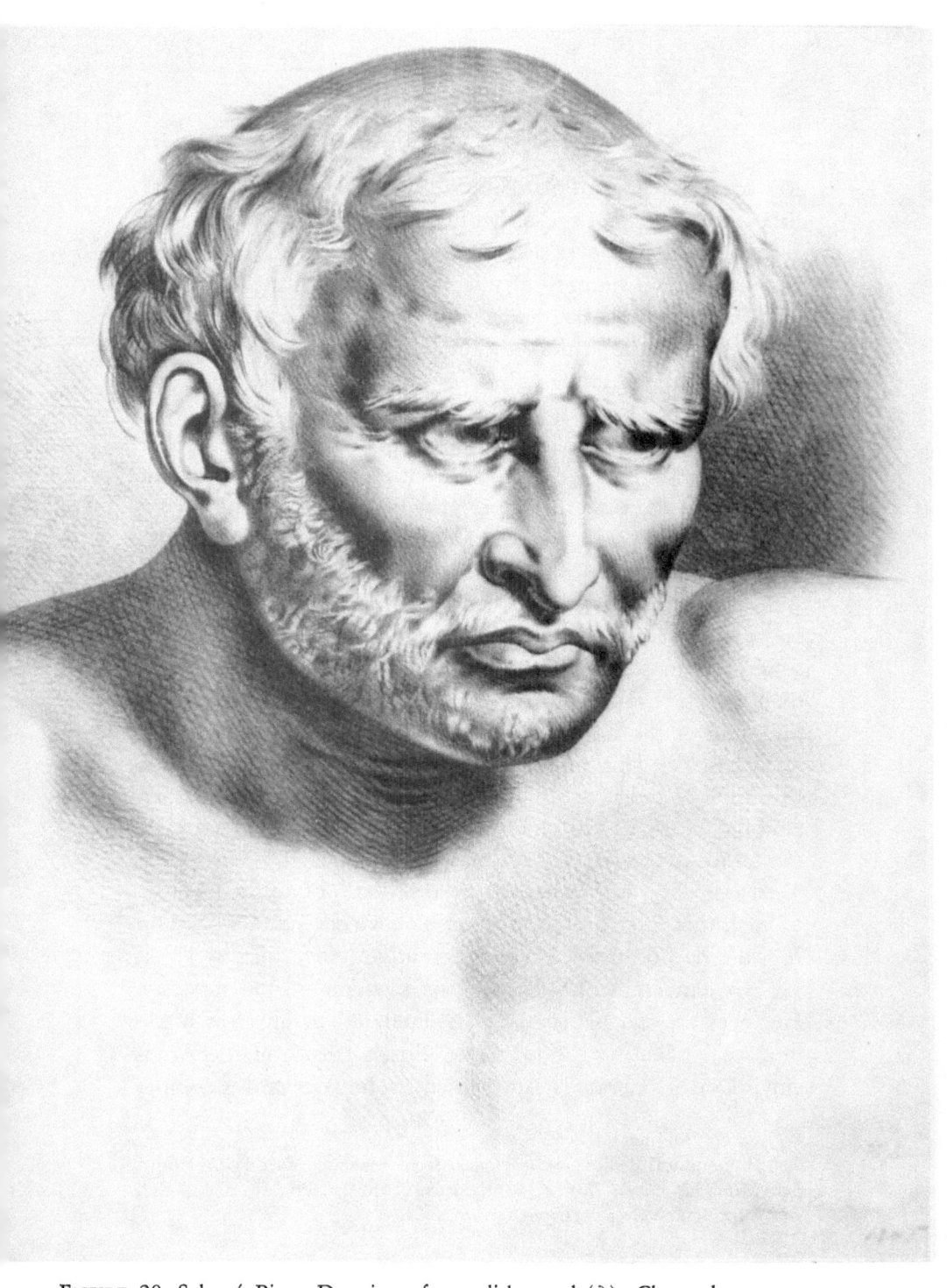

FIGURE 20. Salomé Pina: Drawing after a lithograph(?). Charcoal on paper. Dated 1845. (Photograph by Lola Alvarez Bravo.)

20) by José Salomé Pina was made when this future general director of the school was only fifteen years old. It represents an ill-shaven old man, eyes peering fiercely from under bushy eyebrows. Besides a strength of statement that must be, at least in part, Pina's own, it shows an even more radical departure from classical canons than does the praying figure of Contreras. It suggests a French lithograph, a Raffet or a Charlet, one of the *grognard* types based on Napoleon's epopee.

It is also in that pre-reorganization period that were formed the first artists to have been born citizens of an independent Mexico. All the time they were growing up and learning how to perfect their craft, the elation concomitant with national pride remained mixed for them with the bitter draught of wars and revolutions: "It is exceptional that, in a country just born, sapped by revolutions, weakened by recent reverses, weary of trying all kinds of social systems, a few dedicated men, raising their sights beyond contemporary sufferings, think of the future, and of the fate of following generations." [87]

The first of this generation to prove himself a master was Primitivo Miranda, sculptor and painter, born in Tula de San Antonio in 1822. An elder brother had preceded him to the capital to study sculpture at the Academy under Don Francisco Terrazas, who was himself a student of Patiño Ixtolinque. Once trained, this elder brother opened his own sculpture workshop in Calle de Cordovanes, where Primitivo joined him in 1834.

"His temperament is marked by moderation and modesty. He loves art and his character is untainted by any less noble motives." [88] Sensing the lad's true gifts, a trustee of the Academy, Don Honorato Riano, oriented him toward painting,

[87] Zarco, "D. Juan Cordero."

[88] Biographical details and quotation from Francisco Zarco, "D. Primitivo Miranda," in *La Ilustración Mexicana* (1851), Vol. II, pp. 17–22, with a lithograph after a self-portrait.

which meant at the time the drawing classes and the painting workshop of Mata.

In 1841 a subscription was started by fellow artists, among them Terrazas and Mata, and with the little money that was raised, Miranda was sent to Rome to study under Silvagni at the Academy of San Lucas. There the Mexican soon made good, and one of his pictures was awarded first prize at the annual exhibition of the Italian academy. So elated at this event were his friendly backers at home that they had a special broadside printed to spread the good news.[89]

In 1843, when the Mexican school re-established the Rome pension, its first award went to Miranda, partly because of his merit, and partly because, as he was already in Rome, it would save the institution half the expense of a round trip.[90] This first pensioner of the new era proved his worth by shipping to the Mexican Academy compositions of historical and religious significance that were greatly admired upon arrival.[91]

Miranda returned to Mexico in 1848. Superseded was the informal setup that he had known as a student, and out of fashion the national fervor that he had shared. The reorganized school (discussed in the next chapter) was already basking in the efficiency of its recently-imported and highly-paid faculty, and it had no place for him.

---

[89] Original in the archives of San Carlos.

[90] Archives, Box XXI, 1843–1869, Folder 1. "Lista de alumnos qe. han obtenido la pensión en la academia de San Carlos desde el año de 1843, para disfrutarla en Europa por el término de seis años. . . .

"Primitivo Miranda agraciado en —— de —— de 1843 con la pension de pintura para Roma por hallarse estudiando en aquella ciudad.

"—— de 1848. Concluyó en esta fecha por haber regresado a México."

[91] Zarco mentions among the copies: a Sibyl, after Guercino; the Magdalen, after Albano; a self-portrait by Velázquez. Among the originals were Abel; Cain; Saint Sebastian; Saint Catherine of Siena; Saint Francis of Paula.—"D. Primitivo Miranda."

Zarco implies that the jealousy of the new faculty worked actively to minimize the reputation and achievements of Miranda: "His paintings have been singled out in the Academy shows, even though they were hung badly and in a bad light. We mentioned something similar in the case of Cordero, when sketching his biography. It could be accidental but more probably a willful effort to slight the works of these two artists." [92] Even Miranda's early benefactor, Riano, because he admired his pictures, "advised him not to sign them because he was sure that the name of a Mexican signed to even the most excellent painting would only result in making it generally considered as of little merit." [93]

Disillusioned, Miranda opened his own workshop and lived on income received for commissioned pictures, with only indifferent success. Said Zarco, writing in 1851:

Though Miranda is not completely forgotten, he is forced to give his time to secondary works . . . cheap portraits and *santos* are what is asked of this distinguished artist . . . At most, a wealthy man will buy a Virgin of Dolors on Good Friday, and nobody at all thinks of acquiring a historical painting or one of difficult composition.[94]

Of interest for an appreciation of the taste of the period are the titles of the pictures which Miranda painted in Mexico, and which were mostly commissions. Zarco lists: "Virgen de la Medalla," "Virgen de la Soledad y Dos Angeles," "Virgen con el Niño" (exhibited at the Academy in 1849 and sold to Don José Godoy), "San Rafael con Tobías" (sold in Vera Cruz), "Santísima Trinidad" (painted for Don Francisco Rubio), "Virgen del Carmen," life size (for General Herrera), and a

---

[92] *Ibid.* (See pages 99–100 of the present work for Zarco's reference to Cordero.)

[93] *Ibid.*   [94] *Ibid.*

portrait of Iturbide (sold for 500 pesos to General Arista).[95] Today, the best-remembered works of Miranda are his romantic illustrations of historical national episodes.[96]

Only two years younger than Miranda, another painter of merit, Juan Cordero, patterned his life after that of his senior. He was a part-time student of Mata, and made his living on the side as a peddler. Cordero also left Mexico for Rome without waiting for an official grant. Miranda's first patron, Don Honorato Riano, kept as close a watch on Cordero's beginnings as he had kept on those of Miranda:

I have knowledge of how Don Juan Cordero, enthusiastic at the sight of the first drawings sent from Italy by Don Primitivo Miranda, decided to undertake the trip to Rome, there to study painting; of how he sacrificed what future he had here in business, and financed the trip by the sale of a piano which, to my understanding, was the only thing of value that he possessed. He sailed for Havana, and from there went to Barcelona, arriving in Rome in June of last year.[97]

---

[95] *Ibid.*

[96] Lithographed by Santiago Hernández, *El Libro Rojo* (México, Díaz de León y White, 1870).

[97] Archives, Cordero, 1*b*. In Charlot, "Juan Cordero, a Nineteenth-Century Mexican Muralist," I tell the story of this artist's career. Now I refer to it only inasmuch as it weaves itself into the story of the Academy. Previously-unused documents add to, or modify on minor points, information in that article. The following list, chronologically compiled and arbitrarily numbered for easy reference, is a résumé of the Cordero material that I encountered in the archives of the Academy:

1*a* *1845, November 19.* Letter from Tomás Cordero, father of Juan, asking that a pension be granted to his son in Rome.

1*b* *1845, November 24.* The Tomás Cordero letter is endorsed by trustee Honorato Riano. (Both documents in Archives, 1845.)

2 *1846, January 24.* The Governing Board grants the pension to Cordero. (Actas A.)

3 *1850, July 30.* Letter from Cordero, written from Florence and ad-

And Zarco wrote: "Alone in this great metropolis [Rome] and without relatives, he enjoyed the unselfish appreciation of General Bustamante, who offered him the means of realizing his ambition, which was to study, and so, in November of the year 1844, Cordero was named by the Government an attaché

---

dressed to the Secretary of the Academy, on sending his "Columbus." (Box XVII, 1850, Folder 2.)

4   *1850, October 15.* Letter mentioned in 3 is read to the Board in session. (Actas B, p. 31.)

5   *1851, February 18.* The Board votes a gratification of 400 pesos to Cordero for his "Columbus." (Actas B, p. 38.)

6   *n.d.{?}.* On "Columbus." (Box labeled 1861–1863, folder for 1858.)

7   *1852.* On the return—"this coming year"—of Cordero from Rome. (Box labeled 1861–1863, folder for 1858.)

8   *1853.* Letter from Cordero. He sends pictures to Mexico, and is named a member of the Italian Academia Scientífica. (Box XXVII, 1853, Folder 5.)

9   *1853, May 30.* Records concerning Cordero's pension; and that 500 pesos have been earmarked for his return. (Actas B, p. 144.)

10 *1853, June 30.* G. O'Brien, Paris agent for the Mexican Academy, queries the Board regarding the expense of Cordero's return trip. (Box XXVI, 1853, Folder 5.)

11*a* *1853, October 31.* O'Brien acknowledges receipt of 2,500 francs to finance Cordero's return.

11*b* *Same date.* Receipt signed by Cordero, and originally enclosed with the letter mentioned in 11*a*. (Both documents in Box XXVI, 1853, Folder 8.)

12 *1854, January 27.* Cordero is considered for the subdirectorship of the school. (Actas B, p. 167.)

13*a* *1855, June 27.* Letter from the Ministry of the Interior to Bernardo Couto stating that Cordero is to succeed Clavé as director of the school.

13*b* *Same date.* Envelope of letter mentioned in 13*a*, with a scribbled first draft of Couto's answer. (Both documents listed under box labeled 1854–1858, folder labeled "Documentos sobre la solicitud de Dn. Juan Cordero para la plaza de Director de Pintura.")

14 *1855, August 8.* Vilar testifies to Clavé's fitness as director, and attacks the qualifications of Cordero. (1854–1858.)

15 *1855, September 2.* The controversy is discussed in Board meeting. (Actas B, pp. 185–186.)

to the Mexican Legation to the Pontifical States." [98] Repeating Miranda's success, Cordero took second place in the annual painting contest sponsored by the Italian Academy of San Lucas on August 30, 1845.

In November of that year the Mexican Academy opened a contest in the three branches of the fine arts, offering, for the three winners, pensions that were to be used for study in Rome. Juan's father, Tomás Cordero, presented a dignified petition to the president of the Board. It stated his wish to enter the name of his son for the pension for painting, as Juan had already proved his worth by receiving a prize in Italy. Pleading poverty as the only reason for submitting his application, the father's request reads in part:

At this juncture, I count on Your Excellency to present my plea to the Executive Trustees of San Carlos that the Government sup-

---

16 *1855, October 20.* The newly-formed government advises Couto by letter that the directorship is to be decided in open contest. (1854–1858.)

17 *1855, November 16.* Letter in 16 is read to the Board. (Actas B, p. 195.)

18 *1855, December 9.* Clavé's contract is renewed. (Actas B, pp. 196–197.)

19 *1855, December 16.* Second Board meeting on the subject, to insure a quorum. (Actas B, pp. 199–200.)

20 *n.d. {probably 1855}.* Couto lists reasons why the directorship should be left in the hands of Clavé. (Box labeled 1861–1863, folder for 1858.)

21 *n.d.* Dates of the Academy scholarships, including that of Cordero. (Box XXI, 1843–1869, Folder 1.)

22*a* *1864, December 15.* Cordero asks permission to hold a one-man show at San Carlos. His request is granted by Don Urbano Fonseca on December 20.

22*b* List of works exhibited. (Both documents in box for 1864, Folder 54, labeled "Sobre la solicitud de D. Juan Cordero que pide se le facilite una galería de las del Establecimiento para hacer una Exposición de sus obras de pintura.")

[98] "D. Juan Cordero."

ply my son with a grant. This I would not ask if my present situation allowed me to send my son what sums shall be needed to follow successfully the vocation of his choice.

Tomás Cordero's request implied also that trustee Honorato Riano, if asked, would back his claim to merit.

Don Honorato obliged willingly, supporting Cordero's application wholeheartedly, and adding thriftily that "the pension given to Cordero will have the same advantage as that given to Miranda—it will economize by eliminating the cost of the trip going over, together with the certainty that the recipient is worthy of the award." [99] Riano's supporting letter also implies that Cordero is already being befriended by Miranda in Rome: "Letters written by Miranda and Don Carlos París mention that Cordero works intensely, that his progress is fantastic, considering the short time he has been studying under the famous professor [Cavallero Carta]."

In the Board meeting held January 24, 1846, the pension fell to Juan Cordero, quite unopposed because all other competing works were admittedly substandard.[100]

---

[99] Archives, Cordero, 1*a*, 1*b*. Both documents are written on one double sheet of notarized paper.

[100] Archives, Cordero, 2. Minutes concerning the granting of the pension to Cordero read: "On January 24, 1846, the Trustees met in the Board room of the Academy to allocate the grants for Rome. In addition to considering the painters of the pictures which were presented to the Board, the Board also took into account as a contestant Don Juan Cordero, actually residing in Rome. Reports from professors just returned [from Rome] state that he obtained second prize from the Roman Academy for a figure painting in oil, done from life. This, being about what is expected of contestants, was sufficient to fulfill the necessary requisites. Unanimously, the Board named Cordero as recipient of the grant in painting."

Originally, the pension was to last for six years, beginning on January 1, 1846, with an annual stipend of 666 pesos, 5 reales, 4 gramos, according to Riano's calculations. Actually, however, Cordero received it for close to eight years.

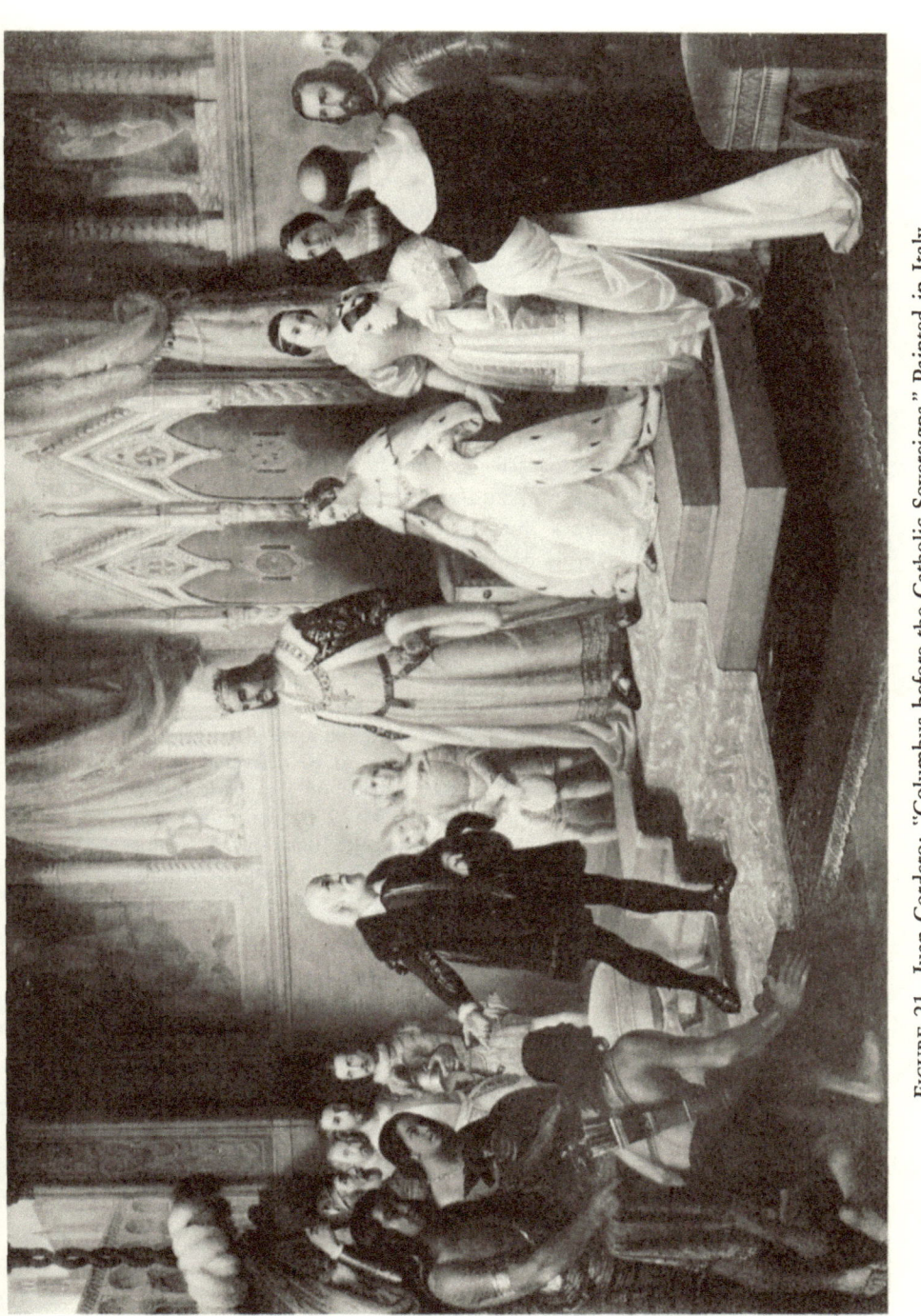

FIGURE 21. Juan Cordero: "Columbus before the Catholic Sovereigns." Painted in Italy. Inscribed "To the Academy of San Carlos of Mexico, as a testimonial of my gratitude. J. Cordero. Rome, 1850." (Gaud Foto.)

The first important picture that Cordero sent back home in partial fulfillment of the terms of his pension was "Columbus before the Catholic Sovereigns" (Fig. 21). Dated July 30, 1850, a letter written by the artist from Florence to Don Manuel de Bonilla, secretary of the Mexican Academy, gave this and other news:

The subject matter that I chose to paint is of interest to the whole world and especially to Americans and Europeans . . . Though it may appear foolhardy when coming from a beginner, I have pledged the poor tribute of my most inadequate brush to the deathless memory of this historical event . . . I would have finished the picture, begun a year and a half ago, and sent it before this, but I had to stop work during all the time that the siege of Rome lasted . . . I am now going to Venice to study at this most distinguished school . . .[101]

[101] Archives, Cordero, 3. That part of the letter which describes the subject matter was published in 1851 by Zarco ("D. Juan Cordero"). In the unpublished part, the artist informed De Bonilla that he had been elected a member of the Academia de Virtuosi al Panteon, and apologized for also sending, in the care of the school, some pictures to be delivered to his father: "Because of the opportunity offered, I made bold to pack in the same box other pictures of mine for my family. May I ask you to see to it that they are delivered to my father? I hope that the illustrious Academy, in its goodness, will forgive me for this, in view of the difficulties, complications, and endless postponements to be expected in sending freight from this Peninsula to our Republic."

The nearly incredible delays attendant on sailing schedules in those days are well illustrated in a letter from the commercial attaché in Rome, Sr. Montoya, to Bernardo Couto, secretary of the Mexican Academy. Dated January 20, 1853, it reports the progress of a shipment of art works: "The statue of Señor Tenerani, the painting of Señor Coghetti, and the works of the grantees have been delayed in Genoa since the middle of August. The ship *Grampus,* which would have brought them to Vera Cruz, was not able to leave port until December 30 of last year. The works are not expected to reach Mexico before early March."—Archives, unnumbered box, R. 1831–1868. When the shipment was unpacked, the statue of Tenerani was in pieces!

When Cordero wrote this letter, he was at the zenith of his European career. His "Columbus" had already been exhibited twice with great success:

At the beginning of the year 1850, the doors of the modest studio of the young Mexican opened to let in all Rome, and the most distinguished professors rushed eagerly to admire the painting . . . The renown gained by the picture caused the Florentine artists to urge Cordero to exhibit it in Florence. He yielded to their insistence. The show took place in the palace of Prince Poniatowski, who showered Cordero with all kinds of attention.[102]

No wonder such heady happenings left the twenty-six-year-old ex-peddler groggy. One ever-present feature of Mexican politics is the distinctive slogan with which the party chieftains stamp their proclamations and the party faithfuls their correspondence. When Cordero penned this letter, Mexican diplomatic documents ended with the politically orthodox "Dios y Libertad," and young Cordero, mimicking it, ends his letter with a ringing and truly heartfelt "Dios y Florencia!"

Upon receiving the picture, the Board, noting that it was a gift of the artist and that its estimated value alone was in excess of the amount of his annual pension, voted Cordero a gratification of 400 pesos.[103]

The picture was hung at the Academy show that opened in January, 1851. The same pedantic jealousy that had attempted to smother the fame of Miranda was still at work:

In Mexico, certain people looked zealously for blemishes in the Columbus picture . . . and one felt pity for these men who criti-

[102] Zarco, "D. Juan Cordero."

[103] Archives, Cordero, 5. Minutes concerning this action read: "The President [of the Academy] explained that grantee Cordero had sent a painting whose worth was in excess of his annual grant. As a matter of justice and as an incentive, he deserved a reward. The amount decided upon was 400 pesos "

cized Cordero and wanted to eclipse his glory for no other reason than that he is a Mexican . . . It seems hardly accidental that Cordero's pictures have been hung where they are; purposely, as it seems, in the worst light, in a willful effort at lessening their merit. This is ignoble; it is shameful, and especially as it is the doing of an[other] artist.[104]

At the sight of this and drawing on his own bitter experience, selfless Primitivo Miranda opened his heart to Zarco, who later reported: "I heard him discourse enthusiastically about the works of Cordero, and express his fear that, when this artist returns to the fatherland, he may find himself cheated of the appreciation and fame that are his due." [105]

Cordero's major effort of the Italian period was a very large canvas, "The Redeemer and the Woman Taken in Adultery," which he took back with him on his return to Mexico. Exhibited at the Academy show of 1854, it, too, suffered "the venomous darts of envy." [106]

[104] Zarco, "D. Juan Cordero." The other artist referred to was Pelegrin Clavé, general director of the Academy.

[105] Zarco, "D. Primitivo Miranda."

[106] "El Redentor y la Mujer Adúltera. Cuadro del Pintor Mexicano Juan Cordero," in *La Ilustración Mexicana* (1854), Vol. IV, p. 5. As to the date of Cordero's return: In Archives (Cordero, 21) the termination of his scholarship pension is entered as "Octue. 1° de 1853. Concluyó esta fecha por haber tenido prórroga." On October 31, 1853, Cordero was in Paris, where he signed the receipt for his travel expenses (Cordero, 11*b*). G. O'Brien, Paris agent for the Mexican school, enclosing the signed receipt, wrote to Couto: "I received the two letters of Your Excellency, dated May 31, and the letter of change for 2,500 francs, sent to be used for the return trip of Don Juan Cordero.

"This sum shall be entered in the accounts of the Academy. I gave notice to Señor Cordero, who arrived days ago, that this sum is for him to spend as he sees fit, toward the expenses of his trip."—Archives, Cordero, 11*a*. The artist must have embarked soon after. In January, 1854, according to the catalogue of the Academy show (p. 36), Cordero was in Mexico: "Don Juan Cordero, Mexican artist sent by this institution to Rome, who has returned after completing there his artistic education."

While Miranda and Cordero were working in Italy, eager to add their grain of sand to the monument of a National Art, the school at home had been reorganized, lavishly so, but along lines less propitious to the birth of a Mexican style than before they left it. A note referring to June, 1843, written in the margin of a book of accounts, is first in time to record the turn of fortune: "This was the last payroll to be paid out of funds given by the Government. The following one for July was paid in April, 1844, out of funds from the lottery." [107]

[107] Archives, Book of Accounts, note after the payroll for June, 1843: "Esta fue la última nómina q. se pagó por cuenta de los fondos q. entregaba el gobo. pues la q. sigue de Julio se pagó en Abril de 1844 con fondos de la Lotería."

BACK TO COLONIAL IMAGE

ON October 2, 1843, a decree of reorganization was issued by His Excellency, the Provisional President of the Republic, General Antonio López de Santa Anna. The successful realization of its bold provisions hinged on the availability of much money—as much as the school had spent in Colonial times. This dream became an actuality when Don Javier Echeverría, who was president of the Board of the Academy, became also president of the Governing Board of the National Lottery, and fused the two posts into one on December 16, 1844. After paying all lottery premiums and allotting 3,000 pesos monthly to the Government, the school still had more than enough left for its operation. With the surplus, it soon bought—for 76,-000 pesos—the building in which it was housed, the same one from which, only a few years before, Tagle had been threatened with eviction.[108]

Steps toward realizing the more ambitious provisions of the Presidential decree were now taken:

1. Directors of painting, sculpture, and engraving [will receive] 3,000 [pesos] each.
2. These directors are to be selected by the Academy itself from among the best artists to be found in Europe.[109]

It gives pause to reflect on the vagaries of fame that the names of the Mexican artists who were bypassed by this well-meaning decree are still "in the air" of art history, whereas those of the famous foreign professors who were so eagerly sought after strike no such responsive chord. The task of searching for a general director fell to Don José María Montoya, who was "Agent de la République du Mexique près le Saint-Siège," and thus lived at the hub of international art-making that was Rome. He approached first three of the more illustrious masters—Coghetti, Podesti, and Silvagni—the latter director of the famed Academy of San Lucas.[110] Their lukewarmness at the prospect forced Montoya to fall back on men less well-known, but willing enough to sail for the Americas. These were Anieni, Pizzala, and the Catalan Pelegrin Clavé. Guided by the opinions of Minardi, director of the English Academy in Rome; Schnetz, director of the French Academy; and Cornelius, director of the Prussian Academy, Montoya's final

[108] Galindo y Villa, *Anales de la Academia Nacional,* pp. 16–17.
[109] Archives, 1843 (manuscript).
[110] Carillo y Gariel, *Datos . . . ,* p. 95.

choice fell on Clavé, a deciding factor being his knowledge of the Spanish tongue.[111]

A contract in French, the international diplomatic language, was signed July 4, 1845, by Clavé, and by Montoya as representative of the Mexican Academy. Clavé received that day 4,500 piastres romaines, of which 1,000 were earmarked for the transatlantic trip, 500 for books and tools, and 3,000 as an advance covering the first year's salary of his five-year contract.[112]

While the decree of President Santa Anna was thus slowly becoming a reality on foreign soil, the political panorama at home had changed drastically. Deposed on May 24, 1845, by a triumphant opposition, Santa Anna was included in a decree of general amnesty, but was banished from his country forever. We shall, however, meet him again.

Soon after his landing, Catalan Clavé became the official dictator of taste in Mexico, and with not altogether auspicious results. Mexican painting had bred for centuries a strong religious art, not only because the Church was the major art patron, but also because of the pious inclination of the artists.[113] Colonial Mexican devotion had been brutally sincere; it favored scenes such as that of the flagellated Christ crawling on all fours in His cell like a wounded animal in his lair, with bloody tongues of skin hanging over His exposed naked ribs. In this and similar themes, the Aztec appreciation of human

[111] Galindo y Villa, *Anales de la Academia Nacional,* p. 17. Also, Archives, 1854, Folder 8, a letter from the director of sculpture, Vilar, reviewing the circumstances of the nomination of Clavé. Cornelius, a staunch friend of Overbeck, was a Nazarene, as was Clavé, a fact which must have influenced his vote in Clavé's favor.

[112] Archives, 1845. The original contracts.

[113] For expressions of piety by Mexican artists as distinct from their devotional picture-making, see Miguel Cabrera, *Maravilla Americana, passim.*

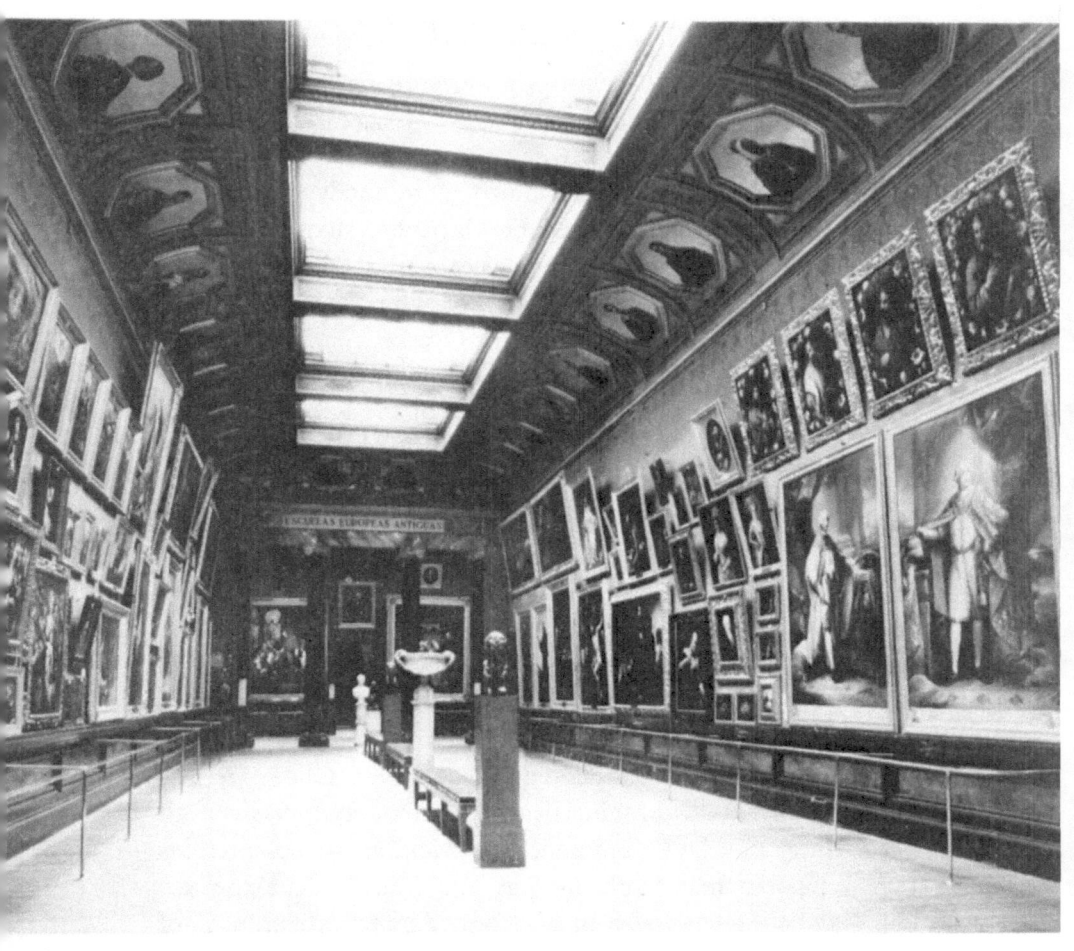

FIGURE 22. Interior of the Academy's galleries of painting, as reno-
vated by Clavé. It features medallions of portraits of old and "modern"
masters, from Giotto to Overbeck, painted by Clavé's disciple, Ramón
Sagredo. (Old negative, by courtesy of Juan M. Pacheco.)

sacrifice blended neatly with the severely ascetic mood of Spaniards such as Zurbarán.

Clavé also was partial to devotional art above all other genres, but his piety was of a much more anodyne kind. Art as Clavé understood it should be Christian, suave, and pulchritudinous. He held in great esteem the theories of the Nazarenes, German pre-Raphaelites who had lived and painted in Italy. Being an admirer of Overbeck, a leader of the sect, and himself a Nazarene in good standing, Clavé despised heartily what he called "the profanities of the Renaissance."[114] Giotto, Raphael, and Da Vinci, among the old masters, Overbeck, Cornelius, and Paul Delaroche, among the moderns, berthed as bedfellows in his admiration. Clavé left us his own "Hall of Fame" in the medallions (Fig. 22) representing great men that his disciple, Ramón Sagredo, painted directly on the walls of a gallery at the Academy, at his dictate. His is a list more temperamentally exclusive than even that of Ingres in the "Apotheosis of Homer."

It became Clavé's self-appointed mission to scrub off Mexican painting what he considered its coarseness. Once carefully sifted, however, this provincial art, he announced, was not all displeasing. In Clavé's opinion, "the Mexican school presents two styles, the first Raphaelesque, and Murilloesque the second," and he left us also in a recorded speech a summary of the history of art as he understood it.[115]

Clavé exhorted his students with compunction:

[114] Couto, *Diálogo,* p. 97.

[115] "Discurso del director de la clase de pintura, D. Pelegrin Clavé, que leyó en la solemne distribución de premios de la Academia de S. Carlos el Día 20 de Diciembre de 1863," in *Documentos relativos a la distribución de Premios hecha a los alumnos de la Academia de Nobles Artes de San Carlos el día 20 de Diciembre de 1863* (México, Imprenta de J. M. Andrade y F. Escalante, 1864), p. 11. Cited hereinafter as *Documentos relativos a la distribución de Premios.*

Dear young men who attend the classes of this Academy with such flattering success, continue with ardor your studies . . . Do realize how soon you will become the champions of the Moral and the Beautiful in the arts . . . Always retain the sublime traditions of Christian art that the great spiritualist masters deeded unto you . . . Rise as did they toward the unending fount of Beauty and, someday, you too will deserve a laurel to match the one that gleams on their brow. To be judged worthy, never slide toward the petty lowlands of human passion.[116]

The new directorship of sculpture fell to a fellow Catalan, Don Manuel Vilar. He signed his contract in Rome, as had Clavé, and the two artists took the same boat for Mexico, landing there in January, 1846.[117] While the changes wrought by Clavé, being mostly of a spiritual nature, remain somewhat imponderable, Vilar's illustrate technically what could have been the method of the doing to death of local esthetics.

Manuel Vilar replaced Don Francisco Terrazas, who was a traditional *imaginero*. Terrazas still worked along the centuries-old lines codified in the ordinances that ruled syndicates of arts and crafts. The Mexican hewed in wood statues that were also gessoed and polychromed. His sculptures proudly displayed, on their wind-blown drapes, toolmarks meant to shine texturally under the lavish application of gold leaf. He thus practiced and taught direct carving from imagination.[118]

---

[116] *Ibid.,* p. 12.

[117] Galindo y Villa, *Anales de la Academia Nacional,* p. 17.

[118] Revilla, *Obras,* pp. 225–226. Revilla, writing early in the twentieth century, endorsed Vilar forcefully, quite unaware that it was Terrazas, not Vilar, who offered a precious link in tradition.

Revilla objected specifically to the toolmarks that remained visible on the finished statue. Also in paintings he confused somewhat greatness with neatness. When young Diego Rivera was studying the history of art at San Carlos, Revilla was his teacher. Rivera remembers how, on a visit to the galleries of the Academy, Revilla would assess quality in a picture by

In contrast, Manuel Vilar was a disciple of a disciple of Thorwaldsen, whose famed coldness and polish he had inherited only at second hand. Clay modeling from life and the mechanically-contrived transposition of clay model into marble statue (Fig. 23) were his trade.[119]

Within the next decade, other teachers were rounded up from Europe to complete an all-foreign directorial staff. In 1846, an English medallist, J. James Bagally, became director of *grabado en hueco,* that is, the craft of making casting dies. In 1853, another Englishman, George August Periam, took charge of the classes of engraving. In 1855, Eugenio Landesio, who signed himself "de Turino," landed from Italy to teach landscape painting. From Milan came Javier Cavallari, in 1856, to teach architecture.

The school building was repaired and cleaned,[120] gas was proudly installed,[121] and a period of plenty entered in boastfully. The trustees who were responsible for the change would have

---

some old master: "Look, my boy! One cannot detect the stroke of the brush!"

[119] The Italian Tenerani was his teacher as well as one of the members of the committee that chose him for the Mexican post. Vilar's gratitude to his master resulted in the acquisition by the Mexican Academy of works by Tenerani—a "Faun," a "Psyche," and busts of President Bustamante and of Pope Pius IX. The eventful shipping of the "Faun" has already been described in note 101.

[120] This was of undoubted urgency. Already in 1822, Poinsett had noted the need for substantial repairs: "There is a very fine collection of casts in excellent preservation, but how long they will remain so is doubtful, for the roof is partly off immediately over them, and the rain falls upon the floor of the room where they are placed."—*Notes on Mexico,* p. 71.

[121] Proudly, but none too successfully. In 1849, *El Album Mexicano* boasted that "the building is lighted by gas, clean, and fit for the purpose it is to serve.—(México, Ignacio Cumplido), Vol. I, No. 2, p. 44. Five years later, however, on January 27, 1854, we find that "the President [of the Academy] admitted that night studies had had to be postponed because the gas meter was not ready."—Actas B, p. 166.

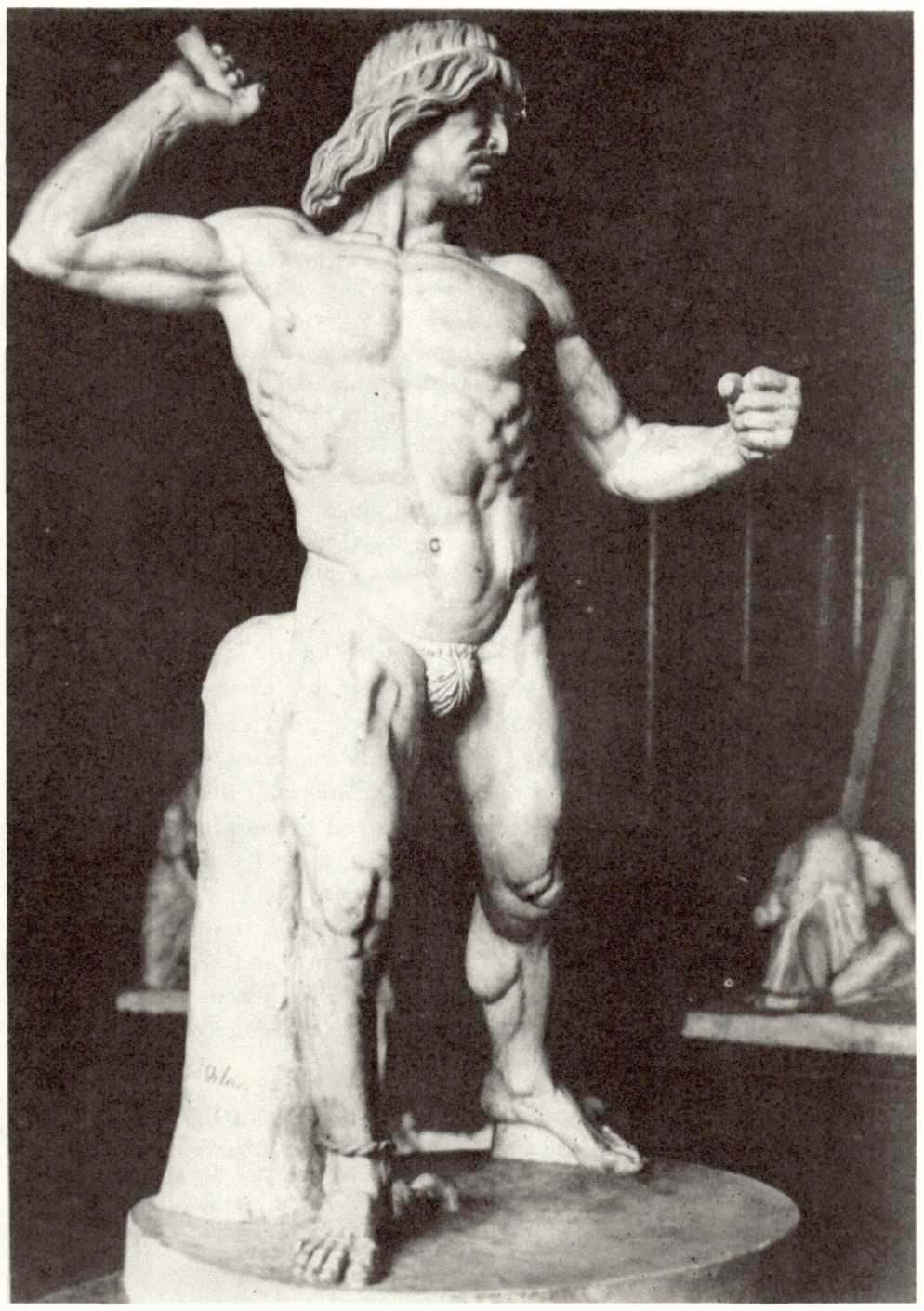

FIGURE 23. Manuel Vilar: Tlahuicole tied to the stone of sacrifice. The sculpture, larger than life in scale, is dated 1851. (Archives of Dirección de Monumentos Coloniales.)

done well at this juncture to sharpen their historical wits by re-reading the clairvoyant passage, published in 1830 by Beltrami, which held that the founding of the school in the eighteenth century sounded the death knell of Mexican painting:

The opening of the Academy was solemnized by the assistance of the Viceroy, together with that of all constituted bodies, and the school was put under the tutelage of Charles the Third . . . But does an Academy result from all that? What is needed is good teachers, and also that allowance be made for national, or at least for popular, pride. The Academy filled up with Spaniards, was made all-Spanish. Its students, the good ones together with the bad, became the only *artists by right,* and Mexican genius receded all into the preceding century.[122]

Beltrami was the first writer to publish a history of Mexican painting—and this thirty years before Bernardo Couto did. In his *Diálogo,* Couto refers to Beltrami specifically, albeit rather disparagingly (pp. 42–43). Yet, Beltrami impressed him. No one has as yet pointed to the obvious relationship that exists between Beltrami's anti-Academy thesis and the surprising remark of Couto (p. 109), made in 1860, that "the death of painting in Mexico is contemporaneous with the establishing of the Academy." Couto was one of the men most responsible for the new state of affairs at the Academy, and was personally responsible for having blocked the bid for power of the nationalists when Cordero was offered the directorship.

---

[122] J. C. Beltrami, *Le Mexique, par J. C. B., ex-conseiller à une cour royale de l'ex-royaume d'Italie, membre de la société médico-botanique de Londres, et d'autres corps scientifiques et littéraires cis-et-transatlantiques; auteur de la découverte des sources du Mississipi et de la Rivière Sanglante, du pélerinage en Europe et en Amérique, etc.* (Paris, Grevot; Delaunay, Libraire de S.A.R. Madame la Duchesse d'Orléans, Palais-Royal, 1830), p. 209.

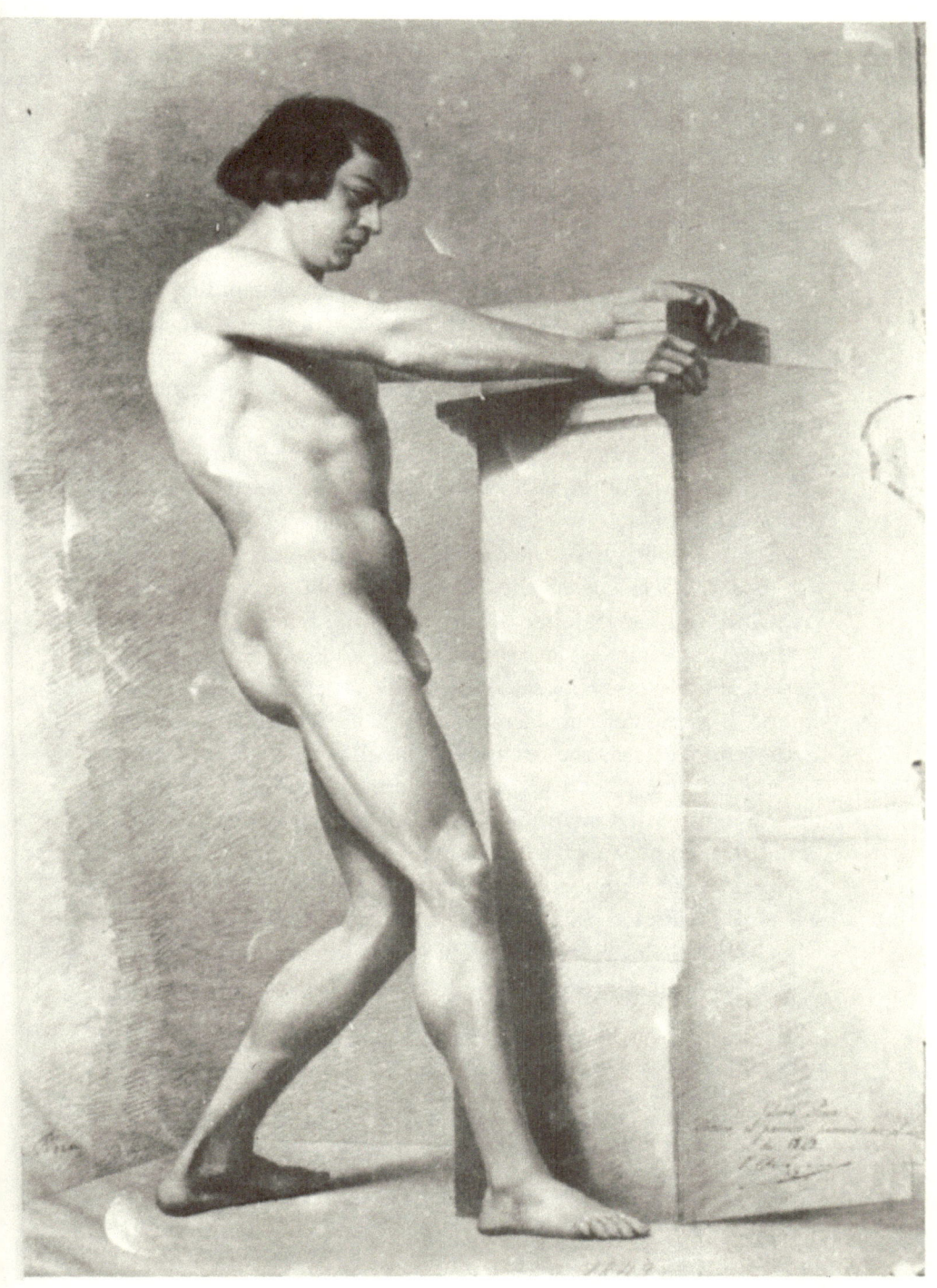

FIGURE 24. Salomé Pina: Life drawing that won first prize in the student contest of 1849. Countersigned by Pelegrin Clavé as director of the Academy. (Photograph by Lola Alvarez Bravo.)

Being intelligent and a patriot, he must have, at times, doubted his own wisdom in the matter. Beltrami's was the only published text at that date that could give voice to these inner misgivings.

The re-formed classes began in the restored building in January, 1847. Clavé favored the use of manniquins, or lay figures, up to then untried in Mexico. They were indeed indispensable for the rendering of drapes, which were in turn an essential ingredient of the ponderous Biblical compositions taught by the director: "Ask from Paris: six lay figures, four of men and two of women, with clothing such as robes and tunics made of soft woolens that drape well." [123] Naturally, Clavé put the emphasis on the study of his beloved masters, the modern Germans of the Nazarene school, unmindful of what incongruities resulted from the shift of locale.[124]

Clavé was doubtless a strong executive. Soon, he had leveled students' works to a safe uniformity, an attainment agreeable to trustees and bureaucrats alike. The "School of Clavé," as these products of the re-formed school came to be known, did not lack merit, and it even developed a few masters. But the admixture of Roman, German, and Catalan undercurrents brand it a potpourri of eclecticism.

There is no better comment on Clavé's teaching than to see how it affected Salomé Pina, a former student of Mata, who became Clavé's favorite. The promises latent in Pina's "Head" of 1845 (see Fig. 20)—done before he knew Clavé—

---

[123] Archives, 1853, Folder 59, in Clavé's writing. Revilla speaks of the surprise that this first introduction of the use of manniquins caused in Mexico.—*Obras*, p. 121.

[124] Archives, box labeled 1861–1863, folder marked 1858. Clavé asks for "a few engravings and lithographs reproducing good paintings and drawings . . .

German engravings by Professors Overbeck, Cornelius, and others $400
French engravings and lithographs $400"

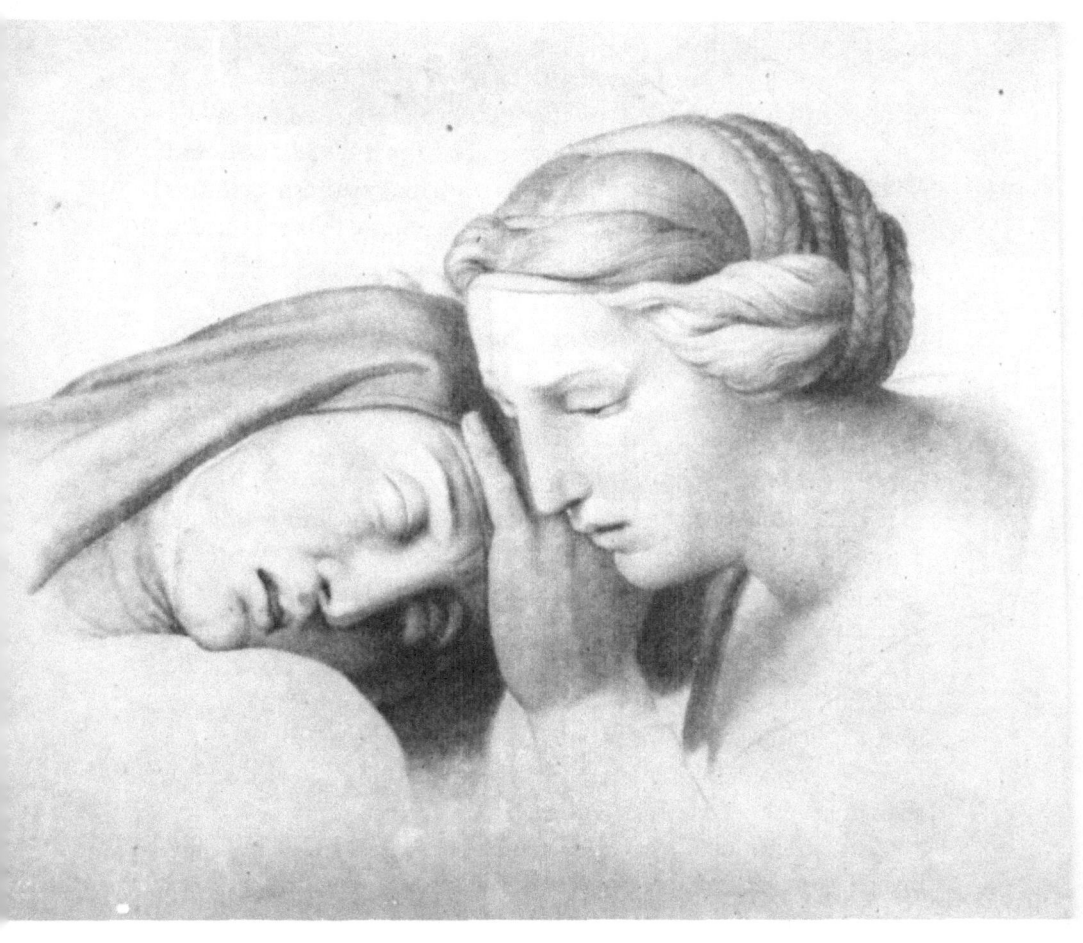

FIGURE 25. Santiago Rebull: Drawing after a lithograph(?) of Raphael's "Entombment," in Borghese Gallery, Rome. Identified by Dr. Wolfgang Stechow. Done under the supervision of Clavé. Dated 1848. (Photograph by Lola Alvarez Bravo.)

were hardly kept in the drawing (Fig. 24) that won him the "Academy" of 1849, which seems to be drawn by another, and a lesser, man. The waxy modelings and shaky foreshortenings are wholly lacking in a certain bizarre strength that still keeps the earlier drawing alive.

A born Ingrist, Santiago Rebull was another Clavé student, one who, in time, far surpassed his master. Drawn in 1848, when the artist was nineteen, a group of heads of holy women (Fig. 25), from Raphael's "Entombment," already exhibits a purity of outline that presages that of his later work. The chiaroscuro rendering that earned the first prize for Rebull that same year still shows, under defacing stains and rubbings, a most subtle grasp of values (Fig. 26).

A slightly younger generation of students grew to maturity exclusively under Clavé's rule. Of these, it is perhaps Ramón Sagredo who stood closest to his master. The drawing that he made in 1852 (Fig. 27), after a cast, is so similar in facture to the "Academy" of Pina as to leave no doubt that Clavé was more engrossed in achieving an equable all-over performance than in preserving personalities.[125]

This intentional throwback to Colonial status was not witnessed with the same equanimity by all. It is, in fact, the adverse reaction of the few—amid the general rejoicing—that brings to light how intense had been their mangled dream of a national art. Miguel Mata, still a teacher at the Academy, became the spearhead of a patriotic opposition to the official order. Having held his peace through the first decade so that time might test the new policies, he wrote in 1855:

[125] The subject matter—by its texture, its style, its details—led me to believe at first that this drawing was a rendering of Tenerani's marble "Faun." In checking dates, however, I found that the drawing is dated 1852, whereas the Tenerani statue did not reach Mexico before March, 1853 (see Note 101).

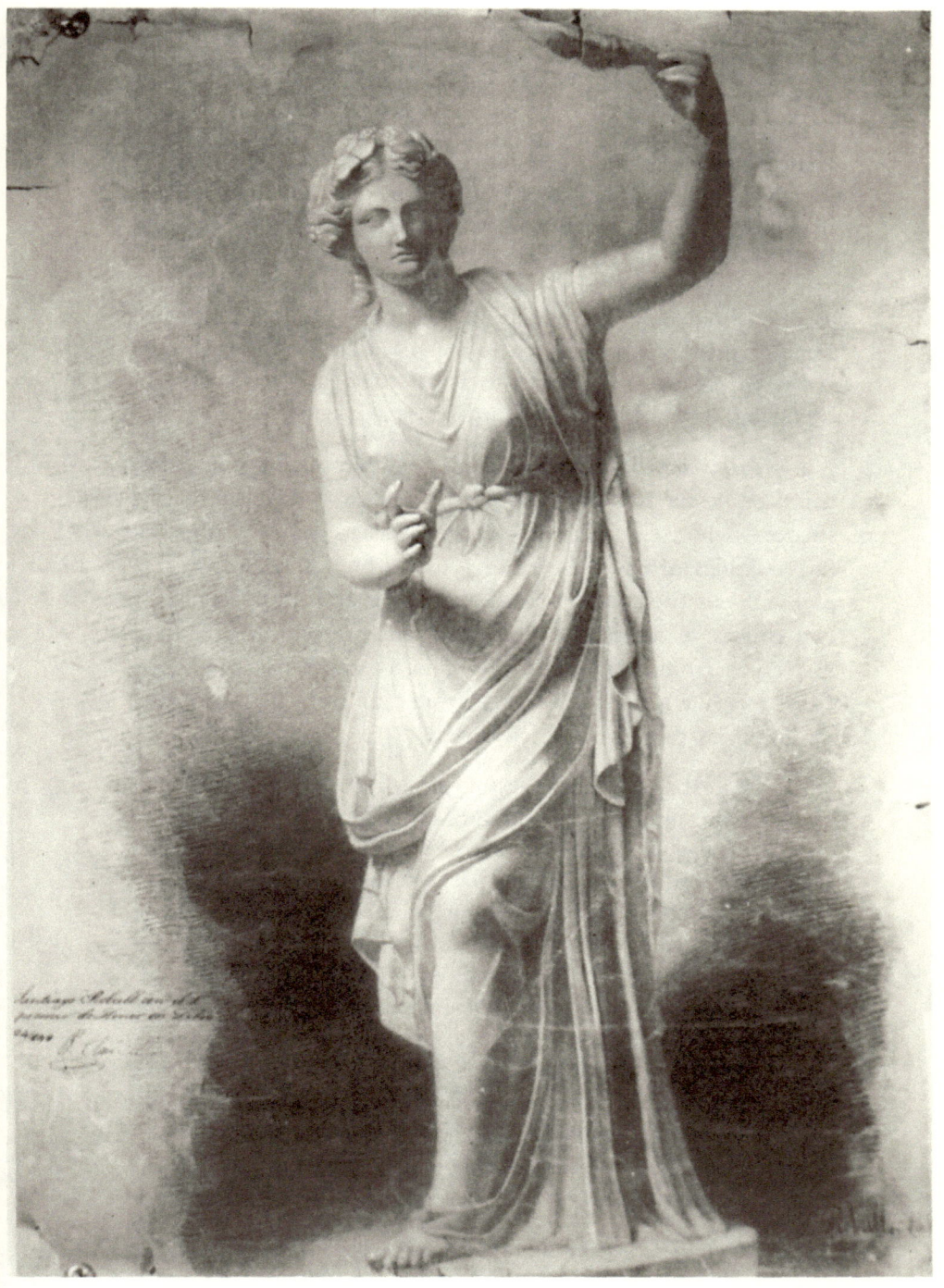

FIGURE 26. Santiago Rebull: Drawing after a plaster cast. Countersigned by Clavé. It received the Award of Honor in a students' contest in December, 1848. (Photograph by Lola Alvarez Bravo.)

These gentlemen arrived here ten years ago. Where are the artists that they have formed? The answer will be the same that we have already heard: It is too short a term to form an artist. And did Sr. Cordero take longer to mature?

. . . Much is made of the works of Clavé's students. They have progressed, undoubtedly, but not so much as is said and believed. Some of their pictures are stolen out of those of other painters; it can be proved how another is but a copy in reverse after an engraving; and yet all are palmed off as originals.[126]

La Ilustración Mexicana was the one cultural magazine that dared brave the established order. It needled Clavé, both with silence—where Clavé himself was concerned—and with elaborate eulogies of those Mexican artists whom academic circles pointedly ignored. The typical passage that follows contrasts two events: Cordero's exhibition of his "La Adúltera" upon his return from Rome, and the show of portraits painted by Clavé, with which the Catalan arbiter of taste had launched his Mexican career:

As regards this most beautiful picture ["La Adúltera"] that has won with justice the attention of all experts . . . opinions remained divided, and some were quite adverse to our compatriot. These, however, seemed dictated by passions akin to jealousy.

It is with works rather than with mean theories that the rivals of Sr. Cordero should attempt to rob him of his fame. Do these men who boast loudly of possessing the qualifications of an artist believe that, to merit such a coveted title, it is enough to show in public a few hundred portraits of average resemblance, with accessories made dazzling by the intensity of color? . . . In works of this type, one copies, he has under the eye what he attempts to imitate; there is no need for imagination, none for creativeness. . . .

Men who were but humble mediocrities in Europe come to our country ready to entice us with falsely-assumed reputations. It is

[126] *La Revolución,* October 30, 1855. Quoted by Revilla, *Obras,* p. 145.

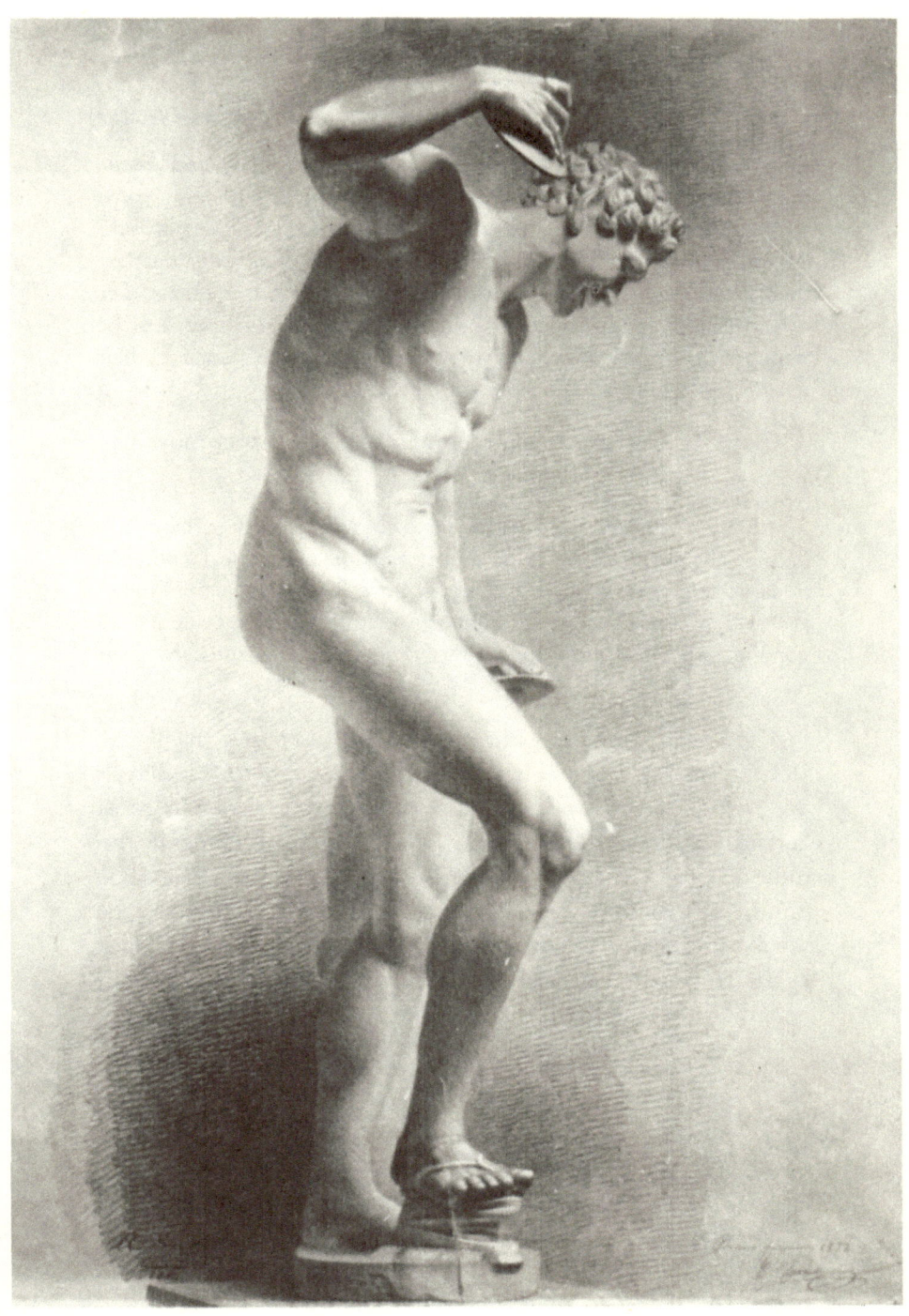

FIGURE 27. Ramón Sagredo: Drawing after a cast. Countersigned by Clavé. Received first prize in the students' contest of 1852. (Photograph by Lola Alvarez Bravo.)

they themselves who write their own biographies, and recite their own glories. . . . Why have these distinguished artists come to a country that neither pays them nor appreciates their works? Are they not sponsored and feted in Europe? Is their only purpose that of teaching us? Is their mission that of fomenting a renaissance of the Fine Arts in Mexico? Can we expect that such an aim be wrought by artists of whom we know nothing? Where are their masterpieces, and where have they been schooled? [127]

Clavé's countryman, sculptor Manuel Vilar, was moved to parry the thrust:

There are a few, far from learned in the matter, who criticize him [Clavé] by saying that, if he has not painted historical compositions, it is because he does not know how. The same people, however, when forced to admit that the pictures of the students are good, advance for a reason the fact that they are painted by their teacher. [128]

The boldest move of the nationalists, and one that came close to success, was the bid made by Juan Cordero for Clavé's post, a bid backed by no less a political power than His Most Serene Highness, the President of the Republic, General Antonio López de Santa Anna. It was, we remember, this same politician who in 1843 had decreed the reorganization of the school, a scheme in which so many now basked at ease. Back again in the Presidential chair from the ignominy of "perpetual" exile, it is credible that Santa Anna had come to repent

---

[127] *La Ilustración Mexicana,* Vol. IV, pp. 716–722. Signed "Luis G. Ortiz," and dated February 3, 1854. Francisco Zarco was the moving spirit behind the policies of *La Ilustración;* in fact, he wrote most of the articles himself, under various *noms de plume.*

[128] Archives, Cordero, 14. The letter, dated August 8, 1855, was written to strengthen the position of Clavé against Cordero in their fight for the directorship.

his earlier decree, having had occasion to witness how in practice its unwise wording excluded nationals from helping to shape the art of their own country.

Santa Anna showed indeed a many-sided mind when he attempted this change of directors at the Academy; at the time, he was campaigning none too successfully against the combined uprisings of two rebel generals, Juan Alvarez and Ignacio Comonfort.

Santa Anna's original letter, addressed "To the President of the Board of the Academy," is preserved in the archives of the school, together with its original envelope. It reads in part:

His Most Serene Highness, the General and President, has taken into account the petitions presented by persons connected with the Academy of San Carlos, in favor of Don Juan Cordero, together with the latter's own verbal representations. Through the highest authority vested in him, He decrees that, as soon as the contract of the teacher of painting of this Academy, Don Pelegrin Clavé, shall be terminated, the post of director of painting be vested in the already-mentioned Cordero, without any other contest or attendant requisite, in view of the fact that this artist's merit is already proven.[129]

The reaction of the recipient of this letter, José Bernardo Couto, was sharp and immediate. Without even taking time to look for a sheet of paper, he scribbled a brave first draft of an answer on the inside of the open envelope that had contained the official order:

Most Serene Highness, I have the honor to put in the hands of Your Excellency the petition that the professors of the Academy present in favor of their companion Don Pelegrin Clavé. . . .

[129] Archives, Cordero, 13*a*. Letter dated June 27, 1855, and signed by Secretary of the Interior Bonilla.

To his care and sleepless nights is due in great part the progress of the Academy.[130]

Actual petitions took a little longer to assemble. The one that is still preserved, that of sculptor Vilar, is dated August 8.[131] What the outcome of this unequal fight would have been is not known, as a full turn of the wheel of fortune accidentally saved the post for Clavé: on August 9, one day after Vilar signed his carefully-weighed argument in favor of Clavé, His Excellency General Santa Anna left for Vera Cruz, ostensibly starting on a tour of inspection. Before his political enemies could catch up with him, he had embarked secretly on the twenty-second for Cuba, and another stretch of exile.

Cordero and his group had lost their battle. Relieved now, the Board "felt freed from the obligation to obey a decree so obviously contrary to law, and one that had not yet been made operative on the day that the Government that issued it disappeared."[132]

All that remained was to get official approval of this attitude. The new President *ad interim* was a rough southern chieftain, General Juan Alvarez. He was reached in Cuernavaca, the provisional seat of the incoming government, and petitions signed by both faculty and students were set before him. This rugged individual, showing more good sense than had the esthetes, ordered that the directorship be won by merit, in open contest, adding gruffly, "His Most Serene Excellency, the President *ad interim,* orders you to forbid that adolescent school students attempt to influence the decisions of the Su-

[130] Cordero, 13*b*. This first draft is dated June 27, the same date borne by the letter it purports to answer. A more evolved version exists also, dated June 29.

[131] See note 128, above.

[132] Archives, Cordero, 20.

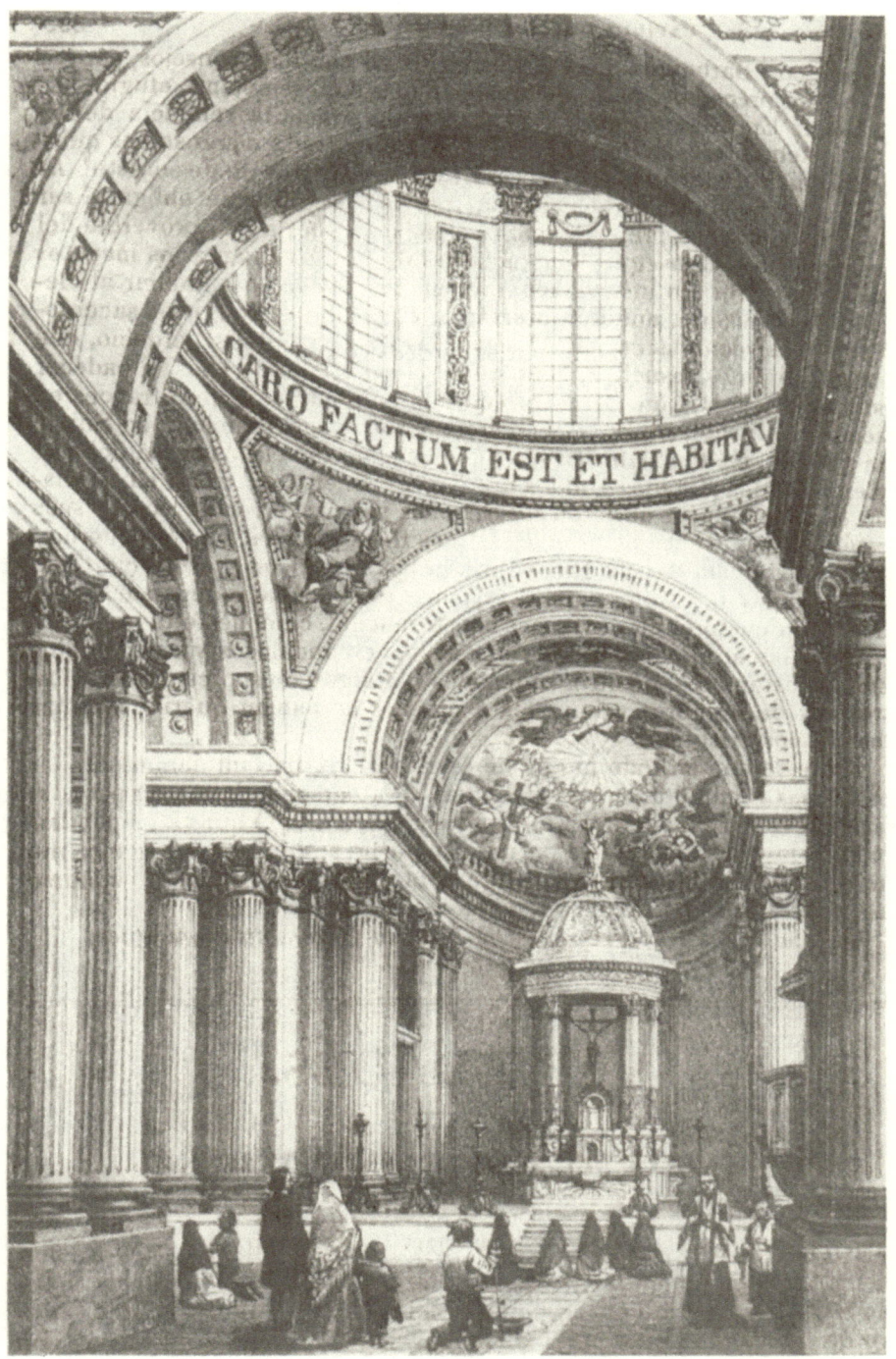

FIGURE 28. Juan Cordero: Murals in tempera in the Church of Santa Teresa. Decoration completed in 1857. (Lithograph published in *La Cruz,* July 30, 1857.)

preme Power. Indeed, He has seen with disgust the role that they have played in this affair." [133]

Instead of bowing to this fair decision, which would have been dangerous to the Clavé lobby, the Board strategically advanced as a counterproposal that Clavé be made director in perpetuity. Then, both parties settled for a simple renewal of Clavé's contract, to run for another five years. [134]

Cordero did not remain down for the count. The three murals that he painted between 1855 and 1860 had made him a figure both controversial and famous (Fig. 28). Clavé was thus forced to answer his rival's brag by entering also the mural field, a genre in which he was but little gifted. The *locus* of his major mural effort (see Fig. 29) was the fashionable church of La Profesa. Clavé stated in a preparatory memo in his own hand, written in the stilted style that was so naturally his own:

Having carefully examined the interior of this church, I came to form a favorable idea of its fitness to receive decorations equal in propriety and magnificence to those of the cathedrals and basilicas that are Italy's treasures, and that have stood for centuries as models of the most correct taste. [135]

[133] Archives, Cordero, 16.

[134] Archives, Cordero, 18. It appears that the length of Clavé's stay in Mexico was covered by four successive contracts: the original contract ran from July 4, 1845, to January 14, 1851. The second—January 14, 1851, to January 14, 1856—was coming to a close when Cordero made his bid for the post. The third, to January 14, 1861, was the sequel to Cordero's defeat. As to the fourth, which would have expired in 1866, the political and military struggle between Reform and Empire rendered it inoperative (see Notes 138, 140). Clavé left Mexico for Barcelona in 1868.

[135] Archives, Box 1861–1863, folder marked 1858.

The most probable date for this memo is 1861. In his *Diálogo* of 1860, Bernardo Couto lists only one mural as having been executed under Clavé's supervision—that of Ramón Sagredo on the ceiling of the picture gallery of the school. He mentions another mural, but merely as a project to be

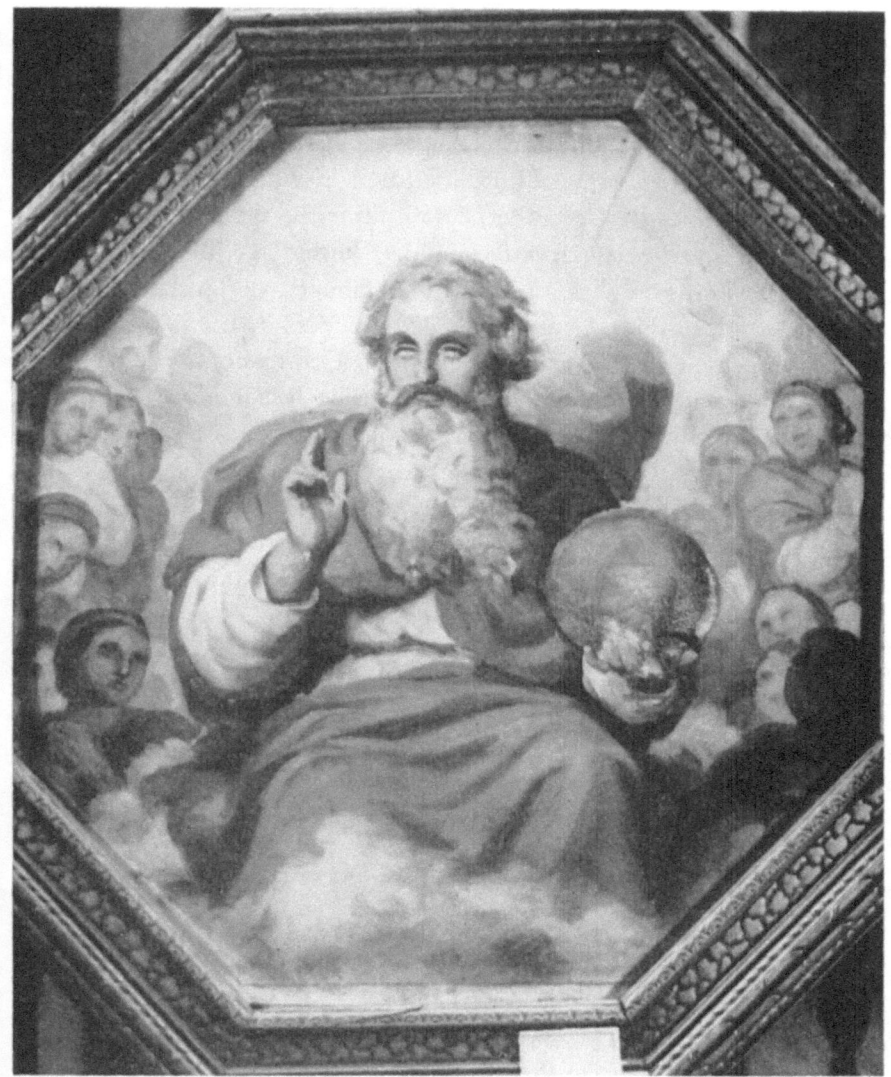

FIGURE 29. Pelegrin Clavé: "God the Creator." Sketch for the center panel of the decoration of the dome of the Church of La Profesa. 1860–1867. (Olmedo Collection, Mexico City.)

Clavé chose to begin this vast work at a most inopportune moment in history. From 1860 to 1867—the span of time that it took him to complete the murals—the upsets that are an expected feature of Mexican politics increased in violence and quickened in tempo. In December, 1860, after the defeat on the battlefield of the conservatives under Miramón, Juárez inaugurated reforms on a national scale. In January, 1862, the vanguard of the foreign invaders landed in Vera Cruz. On February 23, despite the war already begun, Commencement was celebrated with pomp at the Academy. The Indian President presided, ready to distribute crowns and assorted rewards. The harassed Juárez must have presented more than his usually dour mask to Don Javier Cavallari, director of architecture, when Cavallari, in a verbose oration, dwelt on the past splendors of Greece and Rome; after a curious passing ref-

---

painted in the near future in what is now the library of the same building. Couto's silence concerning La Profesa suggests that this major project was not yet contemplated at the time of his writing.

A tentative estimate of time and expenses was also included in the memo: "The dome alone represents work requiring from twelve to eighteen months, to be done by myself with the help of from four to six students. As much time again would be needed for the four pendentives and the absidal dome. I cannot estimate the expense for the work, but the following may help you to an approximate estimate:

One peso a day for each of the six students for each day of work.

Total per month	150.00
Pigments, brushes, each per month	100.00
Scaffolds and gilding	. . . . .

Fee for the Director of Architecture for his help in regard to the decoration, and fee for the Director of Painting for supervising and executing the work: to be whatever you see fit after consulting the Fathers of the Congregation of the Oratory."

The Fathers of the Congregation of the Oratory serviced the church. It was their Father Superior, D. Felipe Villarello, who first broached the subject of a decoration to the Academy Board, following the material damage to the church caused by the earthquake of June, 1858.—Revilla, *Obras,* pp. 183, 195.

erence to pre-Hispanic art as "worthy to rank with those of Nubia and Abyssinia," Cavallari ended with the following pontification:

On this solemn occasion when, as a reward for their exertions, the students are crowned by the hand of the First Magistrate, how fitting it is to draw to the attention of the liberal Government that rules us the fact that this institution is a courier of culture, and the cradle of men who will prove useful to the fatherland.[136]

The comparison of pre-Hispanic art with "those of Nubia and Abyssinia" is typical of the decline in understanding of the esthetics of ancient Mexican art in informed circles at the time. Sixty years before, Humboldt had shown a much keener insight, with his reference to "the remains of the Mexican sculpture, those colossal statues of basalts and porphyry, which are covered with Aztec hieroglyphs, and bear some relation to the Egyptian and Hindoo style." [137]

Indeed, reformer Juárez was not slow in paying attention to the school. He dissolved its Governing Board—which he must have deemed to be but a nest of conservatives—and canceled its lottery, thus drying up the school's main source of income. That he resented also the foreign hue of the faculty is plain from the fact that he demoted Clavé to director of painting, and named as general director a humbler man as well as a better artist, Mexico-born Santiago Rebull.[138]

---

[136] This speech was included as a postscript to *Documentos relativos a la distribución de Premios,* p. 29.

[137] *Essai Politique,* pp. 159–160.

[138] Revilla, *Obras,* pp. 194–195. Archives (Box **XXIX**, 1863, Folder 49) contains an official note to Clavé regarding the cancellation of his current contract as general director, and his demotion to director of painting. The contract stipulated that the holder be given six months' notice in case of cancellation: "The salary of 3,000 pesos shall be paid to you for six months more, as of this date. It is understood, however, that after this, if

The following September, the main forces of the French landed, and a slowly ascending march, fiercely contested, was begun toward the capital. During these tensely martial days Juárez tightened anticlerical measures and ordered that all Government employees sign a protest against the invaders, a gesture meant also against the conservative Mexicans who backed the French, for pious and other reasons.

Sometime in March, 1863, faculty members were ordered to sign the protest or face dismissal.[139] Among others, Clavé, Landesio, and Cavallari refused to take the oath. They advanced that, as foreigners, they felt it improper to take sides, either with liberals or with conservatives. Dismissals soon followed, an embittered Government official remarking of the objectors that "they did not even deign to show sympathy for the country at whose expense they live."[140]

The reduced phalanx of men who believed in, and fought for, a national art felt nearly hopeful at this turn of affairs:

Indeed, we feel that the contracts of these foreigners . . . should be held void. In simple justice, all privileges should be denied them in a country for which they show no love. They are so ungrateful as to declare themselves neutrals, practically enemies, and

----

you wish to continue your work as Director of Painting, it shall be on the same terms as the other Directors, of Sculpture and of Engraving, and with the corresponding salary of 2,000 pesos." Rebull's post combined the duties of general director with those of president of the Board, since the trustees had been dismissed.

[139] Archives, Box **XXIX**, 1863, Folder 66, n.d. "El Gobierno pide se remite [*sic*] la protesta de los Profesores empleados y alumnos sobre cualquiera intervención extranjera."

[140] *Ibid,* Folder 68, March 30, 1863: "Se ordena se destituya a los Profesores Rafael Flores, Pelegrin Clavé, Eugenio Landesio, y Javier Cavallari por no simpatizar con la causa de la Independencia Mexicana"; April 14, 1863: ". . . que se negaron a hacer la protesta alegando la calidad de estranjeros y que no se dignaron siquiera dar una muestra de simpatía al país a cuyas expensas viven."

that at a time when this country's independence is so unjustly threatened.

Surely the same contracts . . . can be offered to Mexican artists, well able to teach the same courses, perhaps even with more precision, technique, and success than did the foreigners now dismissed with much justice by the Government.[141]

These hopes were voiced in April, 1863. In May, the surrender of besieged Puebla spelled military defeat for the liberals, at least for the while. With Juárez in flight, the French army entered the capital in June. A Council of Regents was rigged up—Mexican conservatives who were also staunch supporters of the invaders—to warm up the seat of the Imperial throne for Maximilian, expected the following year.

Faculty and students were again faced with the ordeal of oath-taking, this time by the French-backed regime. In correct political double-talk this "invitation" read: "All the employees of this Institution are to swear fealty to the Sovereignty and Independence of Mexico, and to the laws and edicts of the Regency of the Empire." [142] This time, no untoward incidents seem to have marred the proceedings.

The shifting political signs appeared to point the way of an Academy that was still licking the wounds inflicted by Juárez. The dismissed teachers were reinstated and, on December 20, 1863, Commencement was again held, this time with one of the Regents, General Don Mariano Salas, acting—but only nominally—as president of the Board.[143] In his speech, Javier

[141] "Academia de San Carlos," *La Orquesta* (April 22, 1863), Vol. IV, p. 28.

[142] Archives, Box XVII, 1863, Folder 31, entitled "Sobre que todos los empleados de este Establecimiento presten el juramento de fidelidad a la soberanía e Independencia de México, y a las leyes y disposiciones de la Regencia del Imperio."

[143] Nominally because of "illness"? "The second distribution [of prizes] was made by the Director of this Institution, the Most Excellent General

Cavallari, re-instated professor of architecture, brushed away with an oratorical flourish the memory of the lean days of the liberal regime and gave heartfelt thanks to the present order:

Early this year, the Academy was nearing dissolution. Under the pretext of lack of funds, a group of teachers were dismissed . . . Gathering their students outside the Academy, they managed to give their classes nevertheless, and this without pay . . . With the advent of the new political regime, directors and professors re-grouped themselves spontaneously . . . The Most Excellent Regents approved of the move, and the Academic Body was finally reconstructed in harmony with its Statutes.[144]

Still, the Regents shied at resurrecting the much-needed lottery; they thought that the faculty should be pared down and that school expenses ran too high. We learn these details from the speech of Cavallari, in which carefully-prepared arguments were aired to explain away these divisive points and to change the Regents' attitude. Advance notice of the contents of the speech may explain why Cavallari addressed himself on that day to the chair where Regent Salas did not sit, "owing to a sudden illness."

Further political obeisance also seemed advisable. This time, the once-called Royal Academy docilely changed its current name of National Academy to Imperial Academy.

In a story of the rise of a national Mexican art, Maximilian, paradoxically, figures as one who did much for it. Himself a cultured European, he could scarcely be impressed by Clavé and the other foreign teachers whose glamour in Mexico rested mainly on the fact that they had been trained in Europe. Indeed, in art, as in other pursuits, the Emperor was partial to

---

and Regent Don Mariano Salas being unable to attend owing to a sudden illness." *Documentos relativos a la distribución de Premios,* p. 4.

[144] *Ibid.,* p. 5.

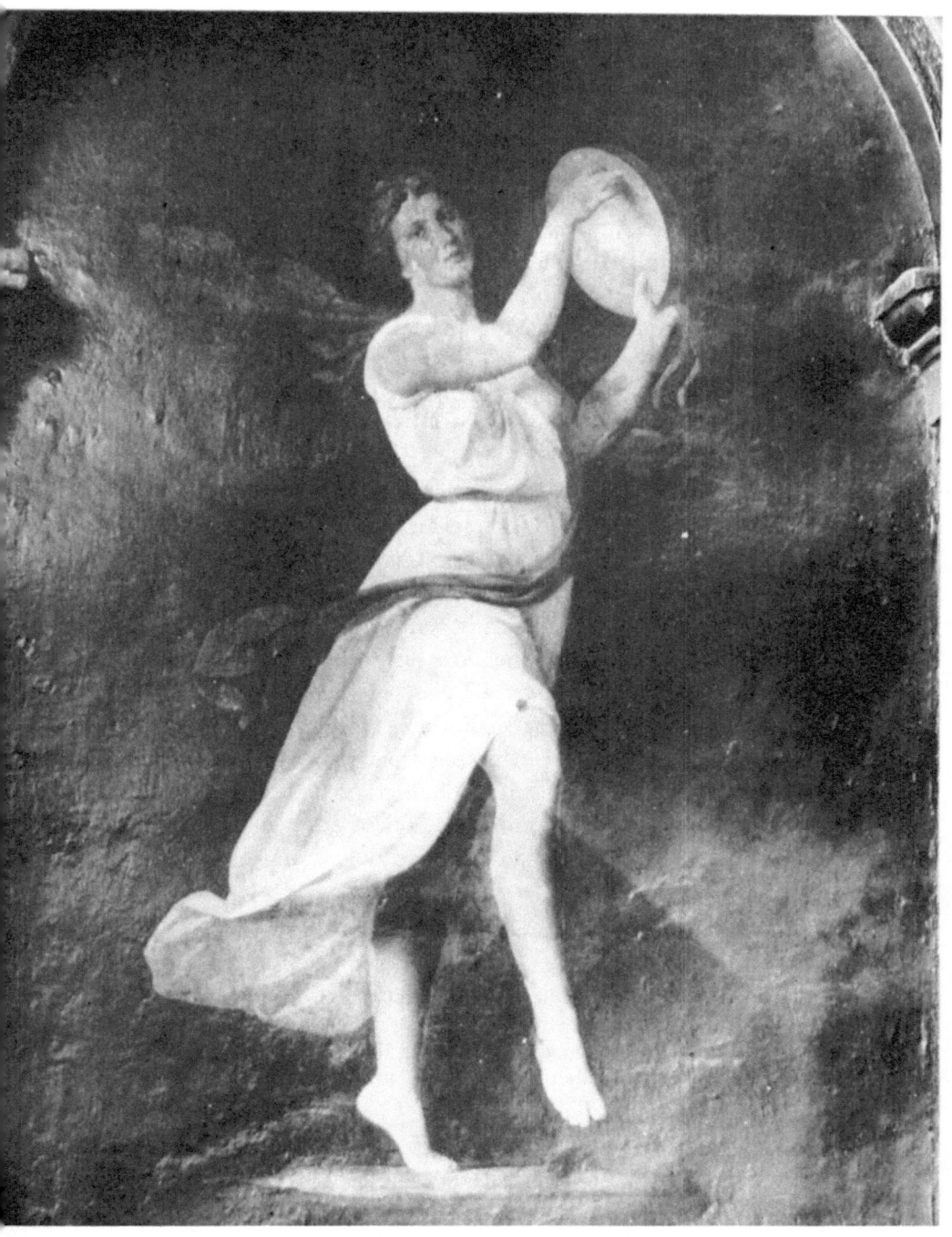

FIGURE 30. Santiago Rebull: "Dancer with tambourine." Mural painted for Emperor Maximilian in the Pompeian patio of the castle. Now white-washed. (Negative by courtesy of Juan M. Pacheco.)

Mexican customs and to Mexican achievements, to a point judged by many as in excess of good taste. Started perhaps as a political expedient, his *Mexicanismo* grew to be so sincere as to reach heroism. After being drilled by the shots of the firing squad and before receiving the *coup de grâce,* the mortally-wounded Habsburg managed to mutter his last word in Spanish—"Hombres!"

Santiago Rebull, who had been picked by Juárez as general director of the school for nationalist reasons, felt it his political duty to resign the directorship after Juárez' downfall. However, he found himself equally in favor with Maximilian, who commissioned him to paint his portrait and that of the Empress, as well as murals for his favorite castle, Chapultepec. These panels (Figs. 30, 31) unusually chaste for their bacchanalian theme, were masterpieces in the difficult genre of chamber murals.[145]

Of Imperial times date the rare early drawings done by a student of Landesio, José María Velasco, who was to become a genuine master of landscape painting. The paper reproduced here (Fig. 32)—a naked man seen from the back—is drawn in very delicate grays, difficult to photograph against the value of the tinted paper. This group of Velasco drawings, despite their subject matter, is at an opposite pole from anatomical display. They are born of a vision that already prefers spatial

[145] Four of the panels date from Empire days. Two others were painted by Rebull in 1894 to complete belatedly the decorative scheme. Revilla, writing in 1902, the year of the death of Rebull, already felt uneasy about the preservation of these panels: "It seems ill-advised that the "Bacchantes" were painted directly on the wall, considering the hazard of deterioration and of fading out. Certainly this risk would have been lessened had they been painted on canvas."

I saw these panels in place in the early 1920's. The figures, in pastel tones on black backgrounds, were but a part of a decorative scheme *a l'antique,* including garlands and vases, in which the dominant note was a Pompeian red. In the 1930's, the walls of the pergola-type of hall on which they were painted directly were whitewashed.

130

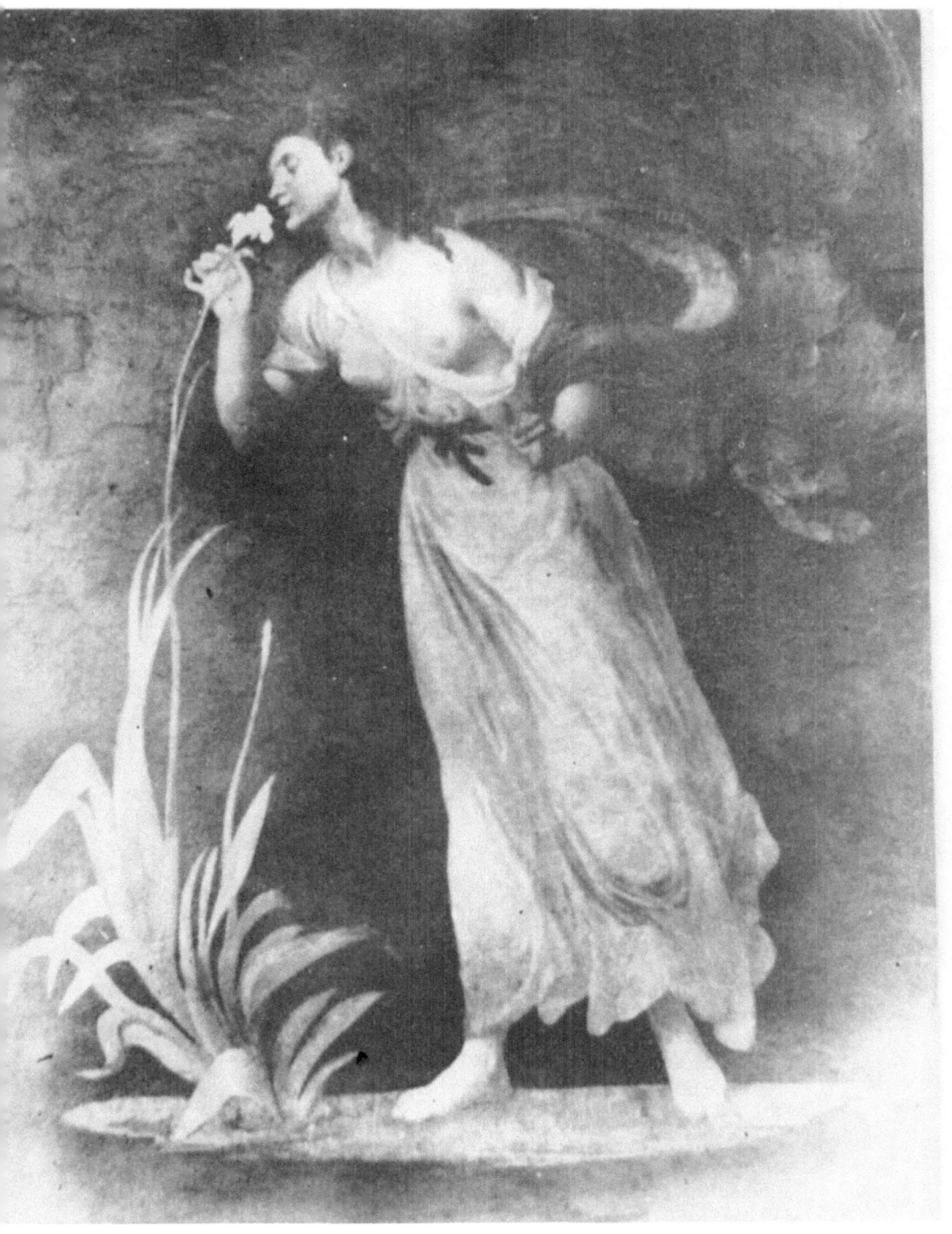

FIGURE 31. Santiago Rebull: "Girl smelling flower." Mural painted for Emperor Maximilian in the Pompeian patio of the castle. Now whitewashed. (Negative by courtesy of Juan M. Pacheco.)

rendering to sculpturesque definition. As such, they point to the mature Velasco's renderings of the Valley of Mexico, where the challenge to his temperament came less from the trees and the volcanoes than from space displayed through silvery light.

Clavé finished the La Profesa murals in May, 1867, with civil war raging in the suburbs. In June, the Imperialists evacuated the capital and liberals again were in power. In accordance with the horror for pomp that marked the reformers, the Imperial Academy was demoted by decree of Juárez, again President, to plain National School of Fine Arts. Nor had Juárez forgotten Clavé's neutral stand, taken at a time when the fortunes of war favored the French. Fallen into disfavor, Clavé left Mexico in 1868, returning to his native Barcelona. Before leaving, he worked hard to keep the school at least under his influence, and succeeded only too well. The directorship of painting fell to his favorite pupil, Salomé Pina, and, through him, Clavé still managed to shape *in absentia* the policies of the school, until his death in September, 1880.[146]

Dated 1886, an adolescent drawing by Leandro Izaguirre (Fig. 33), then a student, and the future teacher of both Rivera and Orozco, shows no slackening in the thoroughness of the academic training dispensed by the Academy after Clavé's death. One should note that, while earlier student draw-

[146] In *El Salón en 1879–1880,* we find selected quotes from the catalogue of the exhibition accompanied by a caustic comment:

"No. 15. Head, copy after Pina, by Manuel Márquez
No. 18. Head, copy after Pina, by Gonzalo Carrasco
No. 28. Head, copy after Pina, by Manuel Pastraña
No. 32. Head, copy after Pina, by Manuel Márquez
No. 33. Head, copy after Pina, by Juan Ortega

Shall the students fill the Academy with heads after Pina? What enthusiasm one feels for the variety in this school!"—Ignacio Altamirano, *El Salón en 1879–1880* (México, Imprenta de Francisco Díaz de León, 1880), p. 62.

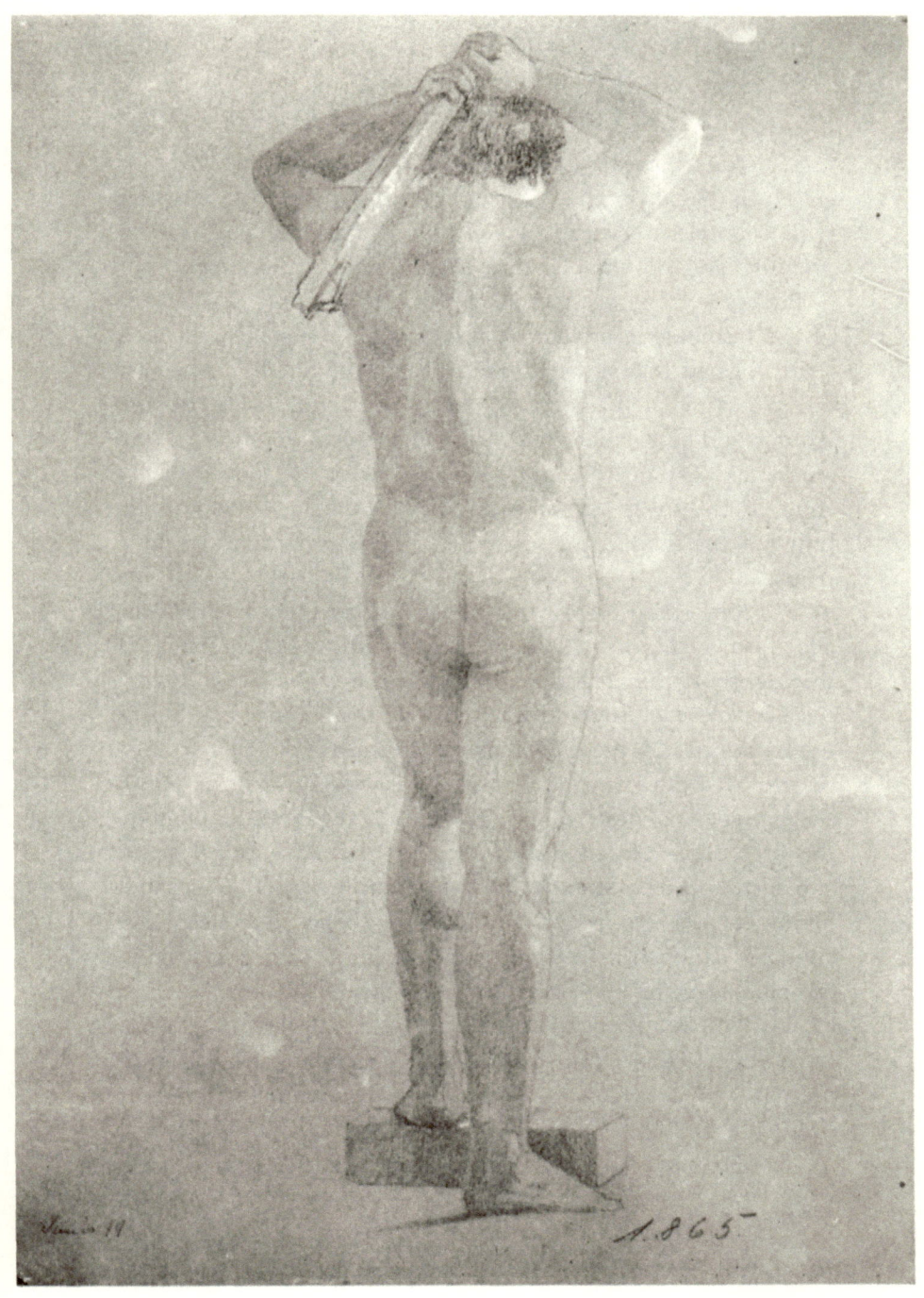

FIGURE 32. José María Velasco: Life drawing, 1865. (Photograph by Lola Alvarez Bravo.)

ings also purported to be a faithful copy of the model, their style was based on that of the masters. Izaguirre saw nature with a "modern" eye, for which photography replaced the engravings and lithographs that trained older generations.

Photography also, digested through the imported influence of the fashionable handmade products of Meissonier, dictated small formats that slowly displaced from the limelight the vast "machines" that had for so long been the pride of the Academy. The small format brought in turn a delight in tiny anecdotes. Typically, a much-admired work at the Academy show of 1879 was a small picture by Ocaranza, "A mouse, by biting a matchbox, has set it afire. He scampers away in a panic."[147]

The long, long reign of General Porfirio Díaz as President added but little to the concept of nationalism in art. Whereas the Habsburg Emperor had respected things Mexican, Indian Díaz looked exclusively toward Europe for culture. The retrograd progress of the Díaz regime is illustrated by two successive Mexican contributions to Paris world fairs: in 1889, the national pavilion was "a restoration of an Aztec temple, the high slate-colored walls rising in impossibly steep steps, and surrounded by strange and forbidding statues of kings and divinities." Again, in 1900, "Today, as befits a modern and civilized nation, the representative building suggests a modern palace, in the neo-Greek style so prevalent in the Mexican capital [!], the principal façade on the Seine, having a handsome loggia, three principal entrances opening on the quai, preceded by a perron flanked by sphinxes and by luxuriant exotic plants."[148]

The director of the Academy for most of that period, Don

[147] *Ibid.,* p. 46.
[148] William Walton *et al., Exposition Universelle, 1900, The Chefs-d'Oeuvre,* Vol. VI (George Barrie & Sons), p. 80.

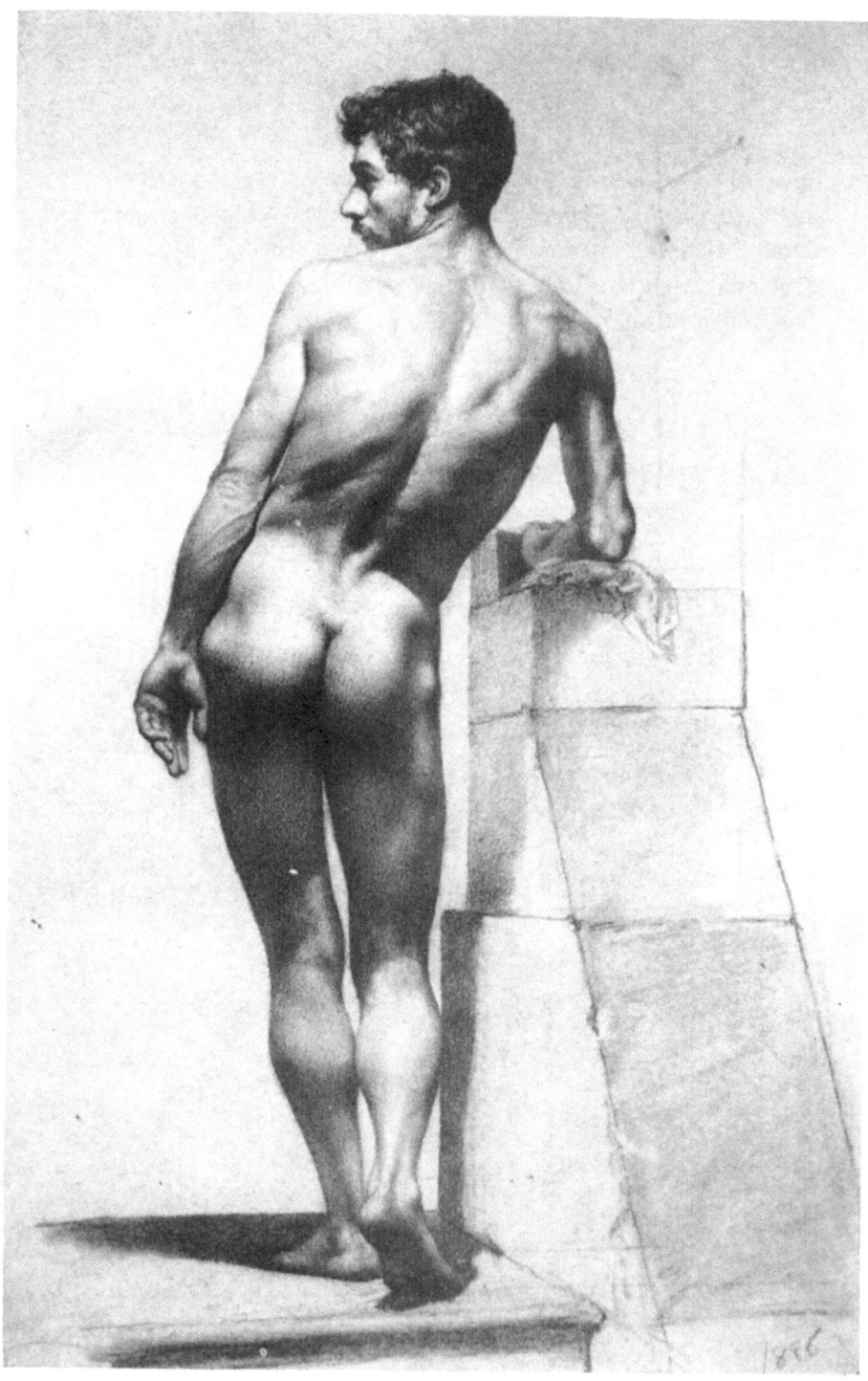

FIGURE 33. Leandro Izaguirre: Life drawing. Dated 1886. In collection of the Academy. (Photograph by Lola Alvarez Bravo.)

Román S. de Lascuráin, followed the lead of the President-Dictator. Again, as in midcentury, the believers in a national art found themselves cast into outer darkness, beyond the succor of official commissions.

MEXICANIDAD COMES INTO THE OPEN

OR the clear expression of a concept of national art toward the end of the nineteenth century, we must turn to opposition sheets that featured cartoons which were in themselves a living art more valid than most academic performances of the period (see Fig. 34). At times, form and content united. The periodical *El Hijo del Ahuizote,* apropos of the Academy show of 1898, loudly objected to its special feature—an imported display of Spanish pictures tactlessly proclaimed as a model for Mexican artists: "We hear talk of what a difference there is between the Mexican works and the Spanish ones. Only too common among us is the impulse to praise what is foreign and to depreciate what is national, and this regardless of quality." [149]

A double-page cartoon retrieved the gauntlet for the badly-buffeted national art. Its theme revolved around one of the few exhibited pictures that had a Mexican theme, Ortega's "A Visit of Courtesy Paid by Cortés to the Emperor Moctezuma." The visitors to the show having left, the two painted principals come to life. They descend from their frame into the darkened halls of the Academy, and, in a fist fight brought on by a discussion of the respective merits of Spaniards and Mexicans, Moctezuma beats Cortés to a pulp. [150]

Typically a wish dream, this episode, dated 1898, coincides with the first tiny signs—at least we can now appreciate them as such—that Mexican art eventually would shake the foreign yoke, more palpably than in a dream. In the collection of students' drawings owned by the Academy, there is a childish copy of a rococo plaster ornament in low relief signed by Diego Rivera, and dated of that same year 1898, when the artist was twelve years old. From the same hand, and slightly later in date, a Venus de Milo and a bearded bust of Homer were copied from the round. With hindsight we can discover in the faceting of Homer's beard a seed of the preoccupation with geometric forms that characterizes Rivera's cubist period. And surrealism could be said to hover over the Venus drawing, inasmuch as she is represented as standing on her head. This unconventional posture, however, was but a device used by his academic teachers to instill in the boy an appreciation of proportions *per se*.

Around 1900 the dean of the faculty was Don Santiago Rebull, the born Ingrist and disciple of Pelegrin Clavé. Since

[149] "El Certamen de Bellas Artes," *El Hijo del Ahuizote,* Vol. XI, p. 75.
[150] *Ibid.,* Vol. XIV, pp. 56–57.

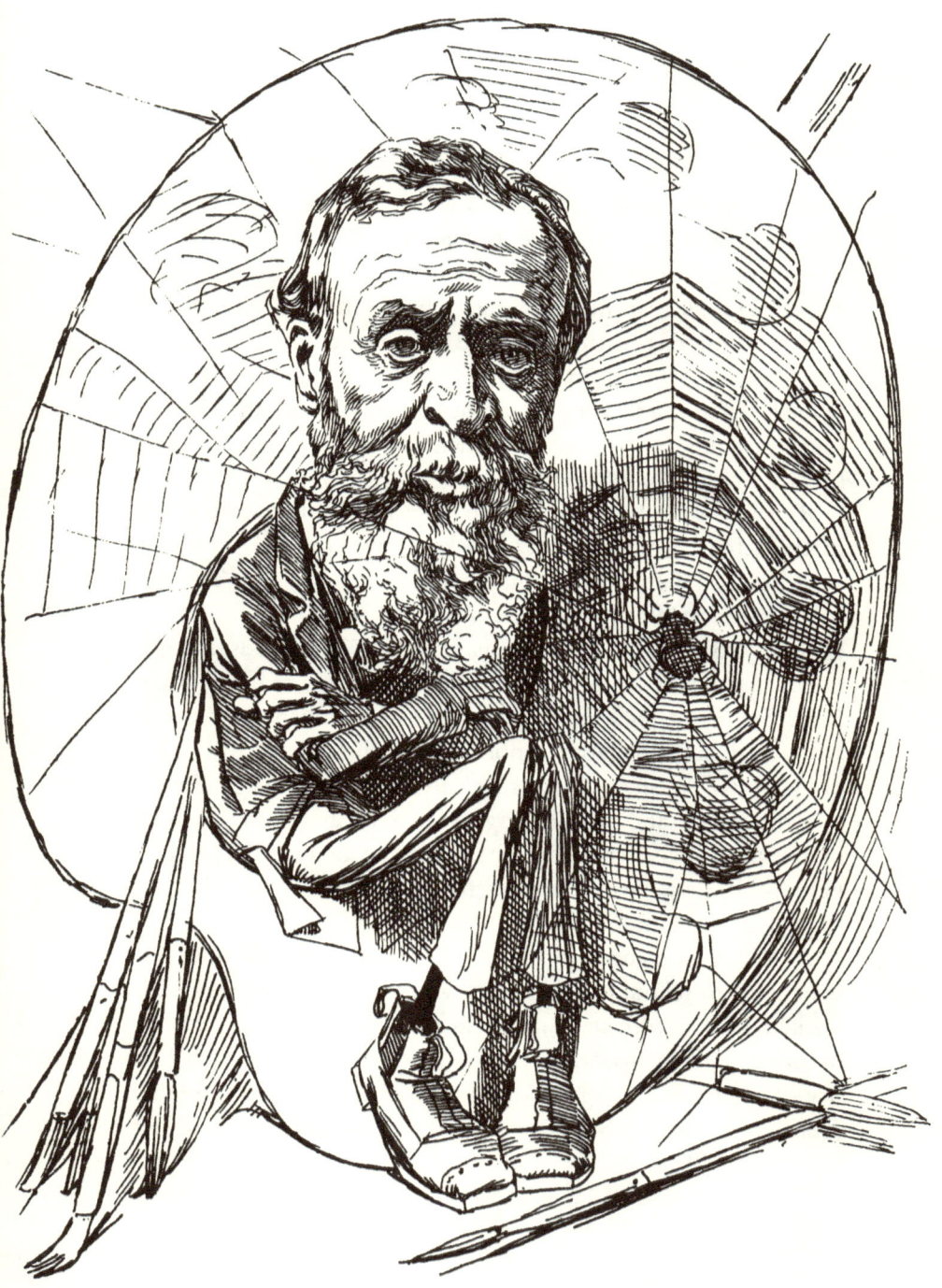

FIGURE 34. Cartoon representing Salomé Pina, here nicknamed Telaraña ("Cobweb"). Captioned "Professor of painting in perpetuity at the Academy of Fine Arts." Printed in the periodical *Hijo del Ahuizote*, December, 1897.

youth, Rebull had shared Clavé's admiration for the religious and esthetic theories of the Nazarenes. The leaders of this forgotten art sect—Overbeck and Cornelius—were still worshiped in 1900 at the Mexican school, though mostly forgotten by the rest of the art world. In affinity, members of the faculty who adhered to the cult grew apostolic beards, disdained fashion, and adopted an austerity of dress and deportment that the tiny salaries on which they raised large Catholic broods would alone have justified.

Rivera [151] soon found an escape from the somber atmosphere of the school. Only two city blocks away from the Academy were the last live vestiges of the Indian city México-Tenochtitlán, which had once been the Venice of the Americas. Streets gave way to a crisscross web of waterways. Traffic loads of vegetables and boatloads of flowers filled the busy canals, brought from the countryside in dugout canoes by Indian paddlers in white and girls in native embroidered blouses and full skirts of hand-woven stuff. Less gracefully, the city sewage flowed into the canals, and neighboring *pulquerías* catered to the thirst of the noisy, busy crowds gathered at the landings. This perpetual folk fiesta complemented for young Rivera what lessons his academic masters taught.

A fellow student, Ignacio A. Rosas, remembers how Rivera came to school in short pants and shocking-pink socks, his pockets stuffed with fearful boyish things—bent pins, odd bits of string, and earthworms that wriggled freely minus the luxury of a container (Fig. 35). Between classes, and presumably more often, the fat boy would sneak out through back streets

---

[151] Much of the material in this chapter directly concerning and relating to Diego Rivera has been extracted from Jean Charlot, "Diego Rivera at the Academy of San Carlos," [College] *Art Journal*, Vol. X, No. 1 (Fall, 1950). It is used here, minus documentation, with the kind permission of that journal.

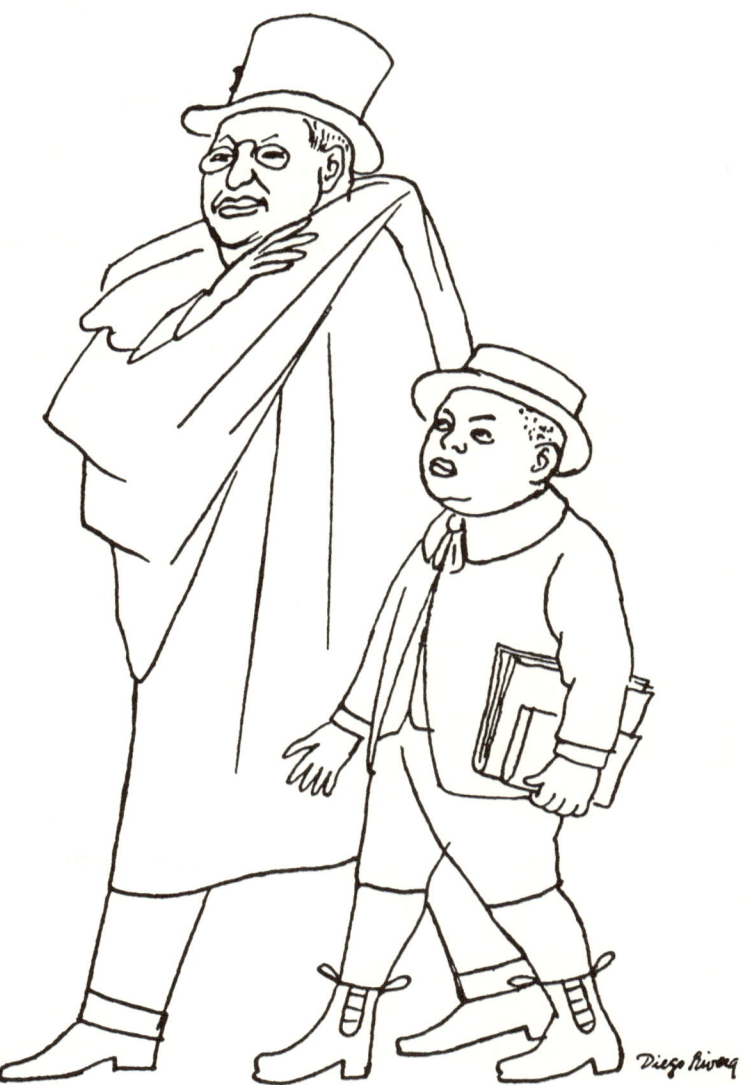

FIGURE 35. Diego Rivera: Self-portrait as a young student at the Academy, walking beside one of his art teachers, presumably Felix Parra. From *An Artist Grows Up in Mexico,* written by Leah Brenner and illustrated by Diego Rivera (The Beechhurst Press, 1953). Reproduced with the kind permission of the publisher.

with low-brow names—de la Alhóndiga, de la Leña, de Machincuepa—and sitting on the bank of the canal, feet dangling close to the stinking waters, fish.

Rivera must have found time to draw too. At the end of the school year 1898, his teacher, Andrés Ríos, after consulting with other members of the faculty, pronounced his work "Very good, unanimously." In 1899, his second year at the Academy, he rated a "Perfectly good, unanimously."

In 1901, Rivera added to his curriculum perspective and anatomy, and the drawing of landscapes, presumably after French lithographs. The next year he began to draw from life and to paint, but not yet from the model. From that time dates a copy in oils after a Bandinelli plaster cast (Fig. 36), astonishingly successful in the illusion of make-believe relief, even when seen at close range.

In 1903, Rivera "took" art history and painted from nature, both life and landscape. The latter class was taught by José María Velasco. The inborn delicacy that Velasco had exhibited in his student drawings was now employed by the mature master to suggest the spatial immensity of Mexican plateau vistas. Velasco's solid teachings spared Rivera the stage of impressionism fashionable at that date in progressive European art schools. Instead, his severely logical approach to optical problems prepared the adolescent for the further rationalizations of cubism. Late in life, Rivera would still tell how the Mexican master introduced him to the classical concept of color perspective while correcting one of his juvenile attempts: "Boy, you can't go on painting like that. In the foreground, you put side by side yellow spots for sunlight and blue spots for shadows; but yellow comes forward and blue recedes, so you destroy the very plane that you pretend to describe."

That same year, 1903, Don Román S. de Lascuráin resigned after being director of the school for twenty-five years.

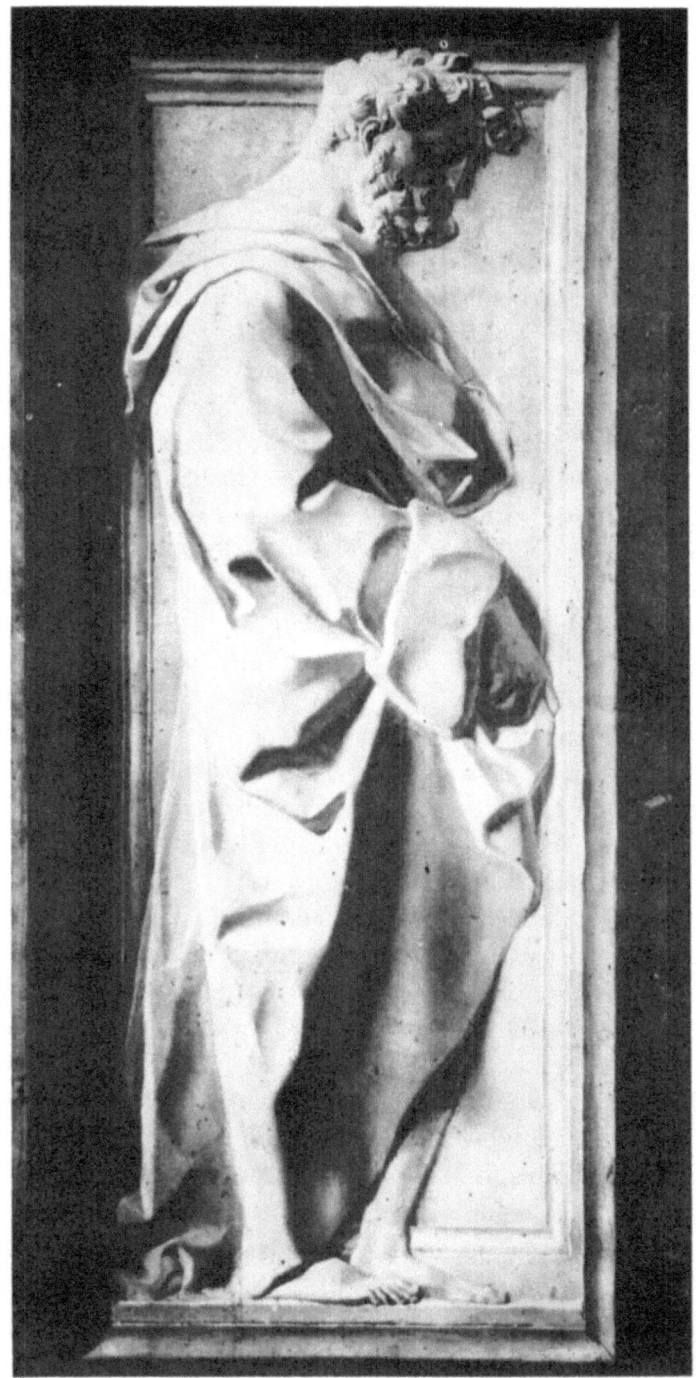

FIGURE 36. Diego Rivera: Painting in imitation of a plaster cast of a Bandinelli bas-relief. Identified by Dr. Wolfgang Stechow. *Ca.* 1902. Collection of the Academy. (Photograph by courtesy of Gabriel Fernández Ledesma.)

He was succeeded by Don Antonio Rivas Mercado, architect and creator of that perennial landmark, the Column of Independence in the Paseo de la Reforma. Rivas Mercado's directorship was eventful. Even before the first rumblings of the great Revolution, he fought in a sort of civil war all his own that split apart the unity of the school. He favored architects, and naturally the painters and sculptors felt slighted. Leader of the far-from-loyal opposition to Rivas Mercado was a painter, Don Antonio Fabrés. A Catalan like Clavé, Fabrés was a newcomer to Mexico. He had just been named subdirector of the school in a personal move of President Díaz, who befriended the recent arrival. His salary of 7,200 pesos exceeded that of the director. His masterpiece, a Bacchanal (Fig. 37), combined the subject matter of Velázquez' "The Drinkers" and the meticulous style of Meissonier. The picture had just been bought by the Mexican Government for 12,000 pesos. Rivas Mercado, at least at the beginning of his tenure, made an honest effort to work in harmony with Fabrés, but the task proved impossible. The school archives bulge with the irate, haughty letters that the Subdirector wrote to the Director to coerce and frighten and bully him into submission.

A historical pattern—illustrated in the eighteenth century by the impatience of Gil with Creole teachers (Alzíbar among them), and in mid-nineteenth century by Clavé's insolent behavior in regard to Cordero—repeated itself. Fabrés failed totally to understand that respect was due to teachers of native birth who certainly were his betters as artists, and besides meant an irreplaceable link in the national tradition. In one of his many written complaints, Fabrés refers to Félix Parra (see Fig. 38), who continued, as he had been doing since 1882, to give for models to his students prints after the masters: "You know very well that, in my system of drawing, approved by the Government so that today IT IS THE LAW, there is

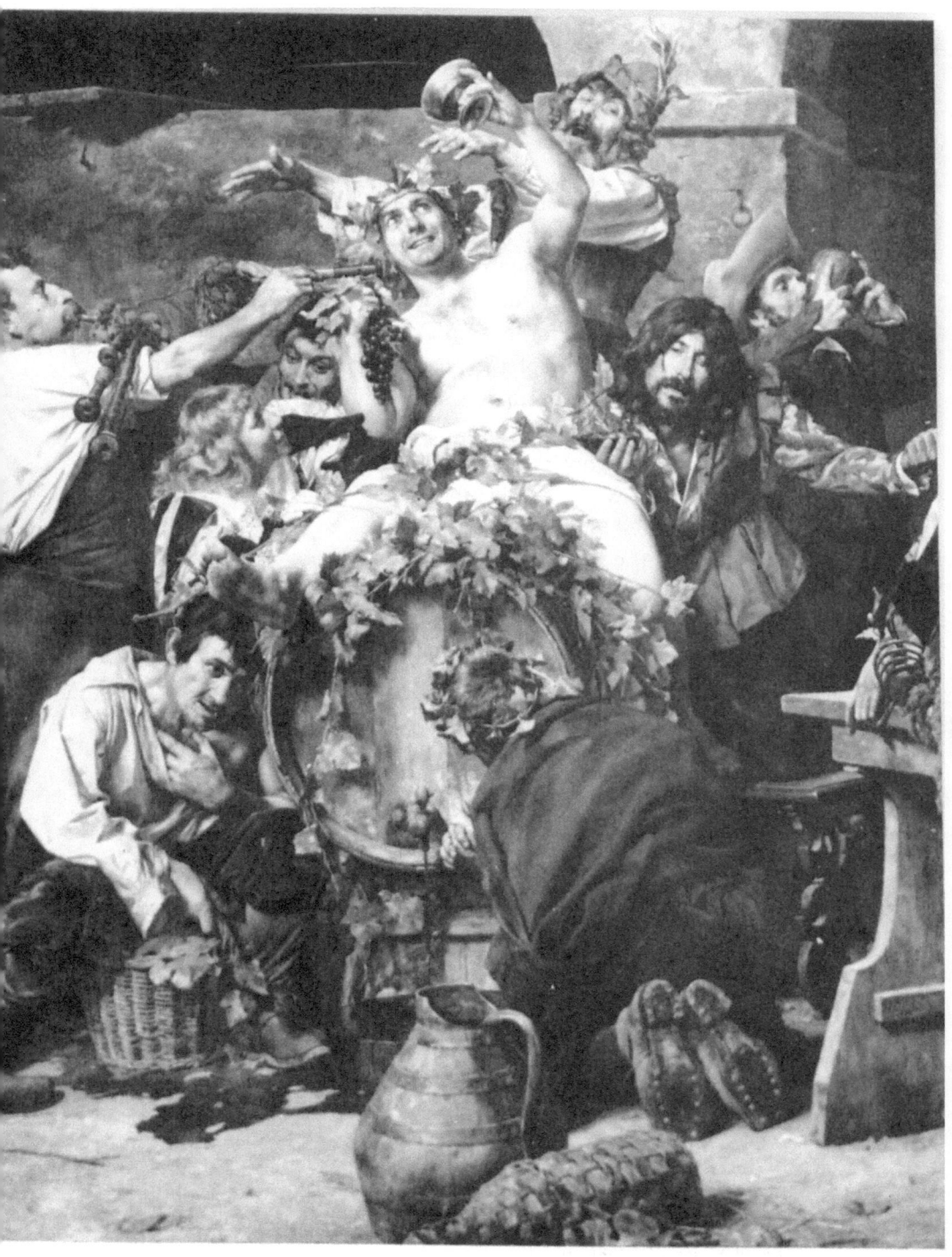

FIGURE 37. Antonio Fabrés: "Bacchanal" (detail). *Ca.* 1900. Negative
by courtesy of Juan M. Pacheco. (Print by Gaud Foto.)

no such thing as drawing from prints. If we keep it for the first years it is only with the understanding that, eventually, we shall be able to replace prints with photographs."

Out of his own mouth, this ambitious man emerges as something of a charlatan, for example in this self-appraisal: "Sr. Fabrés is the discoverer of the fact that, to ensure quick progress in drawing and painting from the model, there is nothing equal to a certain sort of photographs that only he knows how to achieve . . . Now that his claim has been approved, the Mexican School will lead all other schools in the whole world in this matter."

It became the responsibility of the school photographer, Caboni, to put into practice the mysterious method: "Fabrés to Caboni: please be present at life class and at that of costume, there to take, by the use of magnesium and all other customary accessories, the photographs that I shall direct you to take."

The faith that Fabrés put in the art of Meissonier—indeed, considered by most of his contemporaries the leading painter of the age—went beyond merely favoring photographic rendering over the great styles of the past. In imitation of the French master, Fabrés collected old uniforms of grenadiers and musketeers, armor, spurs and leather boots, helmets, rapiers and daggers, scraps of damask, velvet, and cloth of gold. These were deemed the indispensable adjunct to genre painting. Fabrés had brought such treasures with him from Spain to be used in costume class. They became a never-ending source of squabbles with harassed Rivas Mercado. Wrote Fabrés, who spoke of himself decorously in the third person, though with an occasional lapse:

Señor Fabrés reports the following to the Directorship of the school: The individual who models for the class of costume has put the costume I lent him to wear in such filthy condition that he [Fabrés] asks how to proceed in this disagreeable occurrence. He is loath

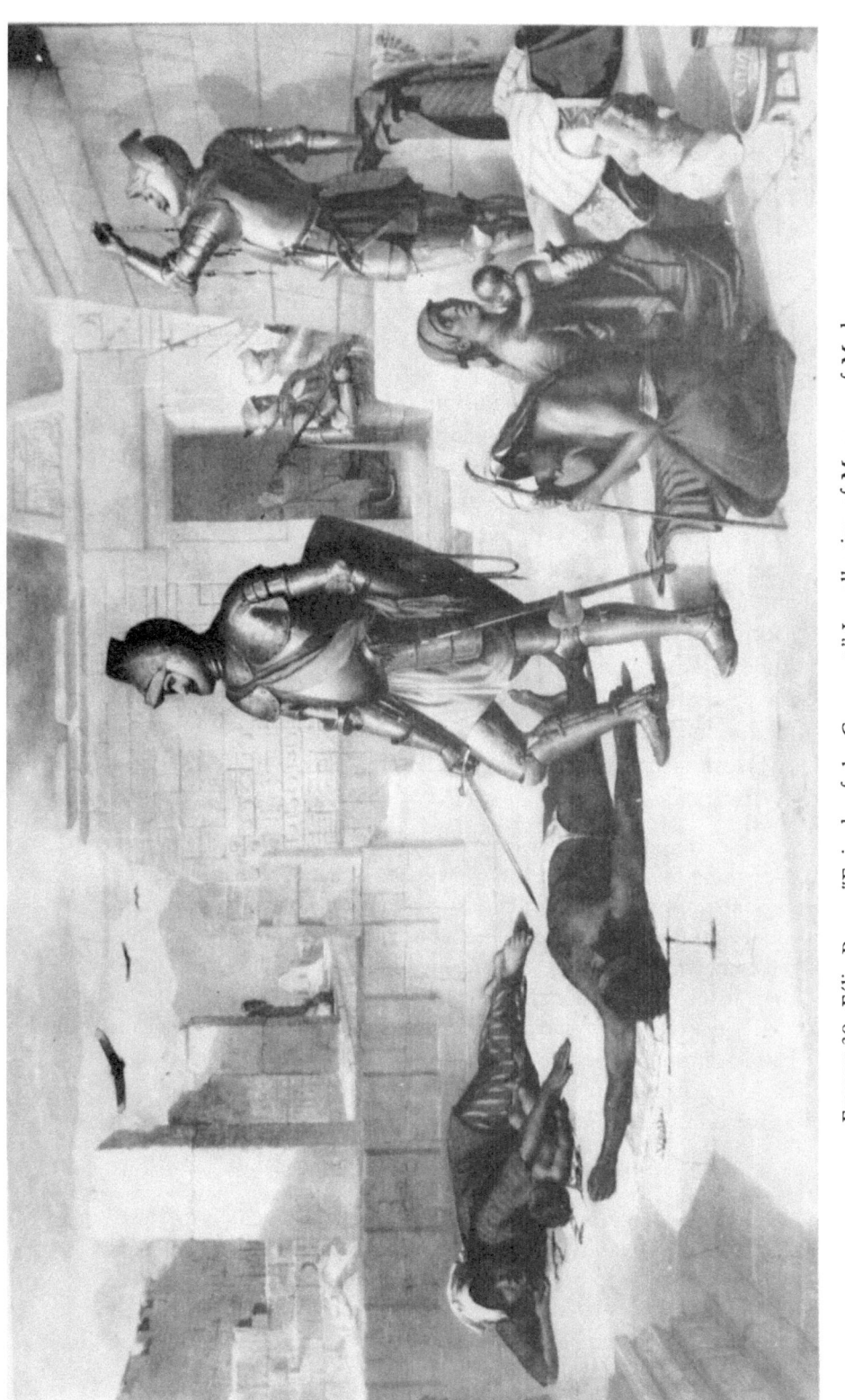

FIGURE 38. Félix Parra: "Episode of the Conquest." In collection of Museum of Modern Art, Palace of Fine Arts. (Negative by courtesy of Juan M. Pacheco.)

to see depreciation in the artistic state of this clothing. To have it washed would impair its quality, and the owner is equally unwilling to let it out of his sight.

Fabrés' ambition, far from secret, was to replace Rivas Mercado as director. His impatience in this respect led to an incident that afforded young Rivera an opportunity for his first recorded act of rebellion. On July 29, 1903, Fabrés gave his students a paper to sign, implying that it was a routine class checkup. As the paper was folded in such a way that its contents were not revealed, the signers had to take his word for it. A majority obeyed, but two of the adolescents refused to comply, saying they would gladly give their names but would not affix their signatures. The following day, Lino Lebrija, proctor of the school, reported to the director: "Last night students Rivera and Gutiérrez were expelled from the costume class of Sr. Fabrés because they refused to put down their names and qualifications."

Questioned by Rivas Mercado, Fabrés gave a heated version of the incident:

These two gentlemen, Rivera and Gutiérrez, not only disobey in everything, but I know, from what other students report, that they also attempt to recruit other boys, equally nonconformist, and loudly proclaim my actions and advice to be no better than nonsense and madness . . . Despite my indignation, I did no more than to point out the exit to them.

If I may state my true feelings, it is that neither may ever again be seen in my classes. As they themselves admit, of what possible use could it be to them or to myself that they be present only as active impediments?

On August 1, both students volunteered their own version:

Respectfully, may we ask how long this punishment is to last? . . . Are we at fault for refusing to sign a paper that was handed

148

to us closed or folded, without disclosing its contents? . . . All that was said is that our names were needed, and we are at a loss to understand why our signatures also were asked for.

Furthermore we suspected that this particular document was meant, as was rumored, for the President of the Republic, in disregard of the Director's orders.

A week later, Rivas Mercado was surprised by a communication from the Ministry of Education that fully justified these youthful suspicions: "The attached petition sent to the President of the Republic was signed by sixty-four students. . . . We answered the petitioners by reminding them that they should obey the authorities as well as the rules of their school."

The enclosed document read:

SIR:

. . . Thanks to your generous initiative we possess a great teacher. After surmounting initial jealousies, he has won us by his vast learning, his fruitful lessons, and the rectitude of his conduct. . . . Alas, Mr. President, we must state that the Director fails to share our views. . . . Could architecture be separated from painting, sculpture, and engraving? This would secure for Don Antonio Fabrés the independence he needs to fulfill the mission that brought him to Mexico. . . .

Enlightened, Director Rivas Mercado re-instated Rivera and Gutiérrez. It must be said for Fabrés that he showed no resentment. In the final tests for his class, while the medal went to Nacho Rosas, Rivera received honorable mention.

The next year, 1904, the breach widened still further between Director and Subdirector. In a huff, Fabrés took his famed wardrobe out of the school building. Whereupon Rivas Mercado complained to his superior, Secretary of Education Don Justo Sierra: "Since February 6, the students have been drawing from the model just as he happens to be; that is, in the clothing of the lower classes to which he belongs" (see Fig. 39).

Whatever may be the opinion of later generations of artists, who prefer to paint the Indian in his white *calzones,* or better still, in overalls, this was dismal news indeed at the turn of the century, and Fabrés was begged to reconsider. Still referring to himself in the third person, he refused to comply in no uncertain terms: "Señor Fabrés, as owner, sole owner, of the costumes . . . feels moved to answer, I repeat, AS THEIR OWNER, that he is resolved not to lend them anymore."

On April 19, Rivera and his fellow students, reduced to the plight of painting Mexicans as they are, humbly petitioned the Director: "Could there be a way to give us the opportunity of studying the costume? Besides being instructive, such classes also were most entertaining. We gained knowledge of the diverse styles of clothing according to periods, and a wealth of color and much artistic interest were added to the model." Rivera, having made his peace with Fabrés, appears among the signers.

Lethargic Rivas Mercado eventually won the battle against the mercurial Fabrés. In 1906, in a letter to Don Justo Sierra, Director Rivas Mercado wrote his rival's epitaph:

It is by now public knowledge that photographic cameras are used in his classes. From now on, Señor Fabrés and his adherents will have to do without what proved their supreme recourse for dazzling laymen as well as for ensnaring their own selves.

His [Fabrés'] incompetence as a teacher should be easy to demonstrate, once he is stripped of his only weapon in the competition of lawful teaching. I refer, of course, to the *cámara lúcida,* with whose powerful help he tricked the good faith of men unversed in matters of art.

In that year, 1906, the Academy held a group exhibition of the work of students pensioned to study in Europe. Rivera

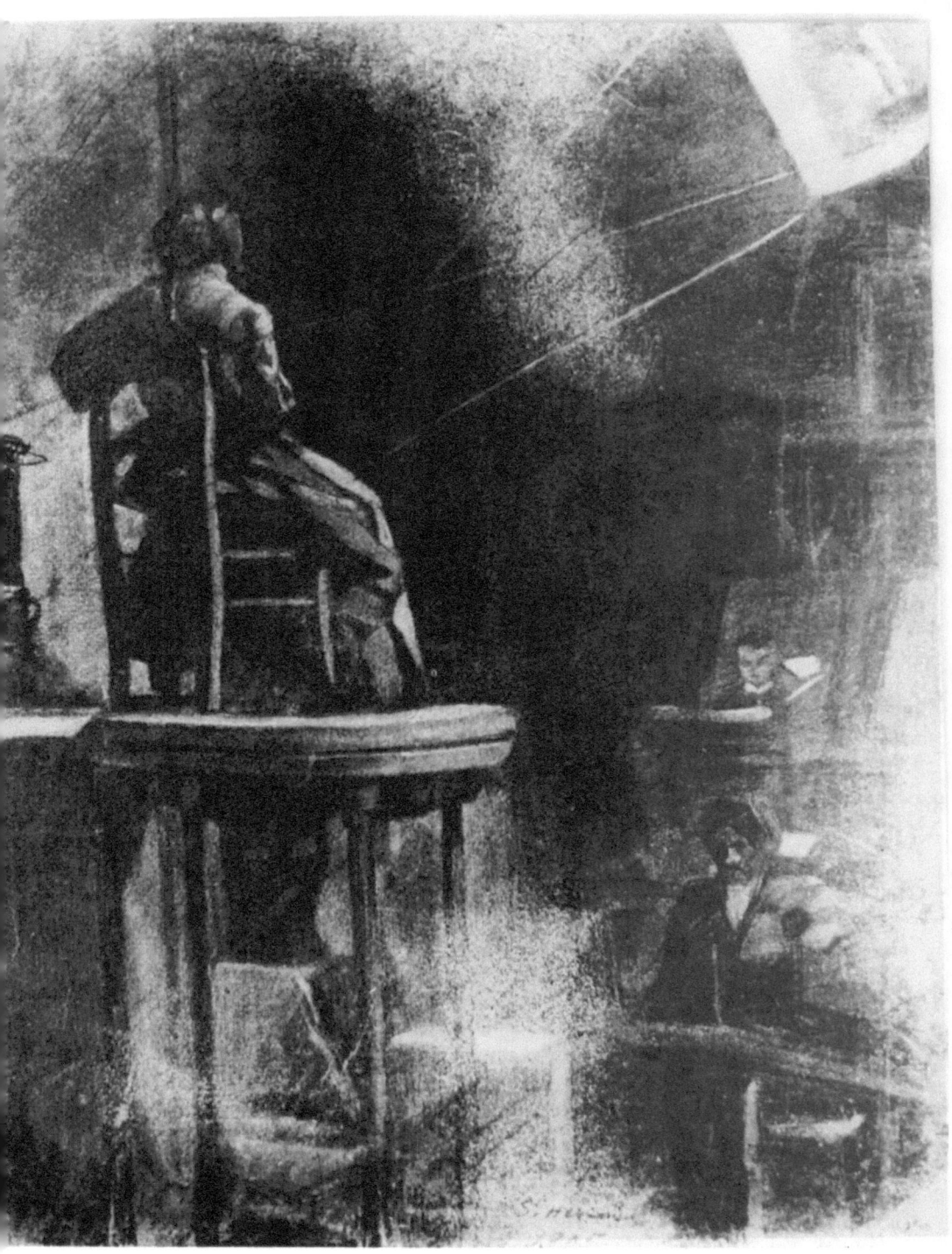

FIGURE 39. Saturnino Herrán: Charcoal drawing. A classroom of costumed model at the Academy in 1905. In collection of the school. (Photograph by Lola Alvarez Bravo.)

had just been pensioned by the Governor of his native State of Vera Cruz, General Teodoro Dehesa. Before leaving for Spain, he displayed in this group show the landscapes he had painted under Velasco.

Exit Rivera. Enter José Clemente Orozco.[152] Though older than Rivera by four years, Orozco came to art later than his compatriot, having first oriented his career to that of agricultural engineer. Rivera had been trained to art from childhood; for Orozco, up to the time he became associated with the Academy, art had been no more than an avocation. The first mention of Orozco as a student in the archives of the school is in 1906, the year Rivera left for Europe. Fabrés, despite his downgrading, was still a member of the faculty. He gave two night classes, one of the nude and one of the costumed model, but attended them only halfheartedly. Oftentimes he failed to come, or left before time. The model would leave early, too. A few students would follow the model and, soon after, the class would exit *in toto*.

The proctor, Lino Lebrija, stolidly stood guard by the main entrance, a living reproach to the slackness of the students. Afterwards, he penned his reports to Director Rivas Mercado:

Disobeying your orders, two of the students of Professor Antonio Fabrés started a rumpus the evening of the seventh of the current month, May, 1906. Its outcome was the total exit of the students of these two classes, with the proctor and his aids helpless to restore order. . . .

Such a scene was re-enacted yesterday, and student García Núñez, while scuffling with the proctor, tore loose the bellpull of the door. . . .

[152] For material concerning Orozco and Alfaro Siqueiros, I am again indebted to the [College] *Art Journal* for permission to extract from Jean Charlot, "Orozco and Siqueiros at the Academy of San Carlos," Vol. X, No. 4 (Summer, 1951).

The unruly Núñez and a fellow agitator were expelled for fifteen days. A petition in their favor, signed by ten of Fabrés' students, Orozco among them, was forwarded to the Director:

It is with intense surprise that we learned of the order to expell from the school our fellow students because they left before time . . . If we left, it was only because there was no model—he was gone by 8:00 P.M.—and so there was no further purpose in keeping to the classroom. If these two students deserve punishment, then we shall consider ourselves expelled together with them, that is, all of us who left the building that night. . . .

By 1910, Orozco was referred to as a senior student of life-class when his contest drawing was adjudged *hors-concours* (ineligible for the competition), a rating which implies that he had previously received his full share of honors.

The year 1910 was Centennial Year, with many festivities planned for September, to commemorate Hidalgo's uprising and Mexico's political independence from Spain. With a kind of surrealistic illogic, President Díaz ruled that a gigantic display of contemporary Spanish art should add fitting gloss to the celebration. Toward this end 35,000 pesos were allotted, with a specially-constructed exhibition building thrown in.

Young Mexican artists, most of them students of the Academy, naturally were nonplussed. They decided to put up their own display of national art, either forgotten or willfully slighted by the Presidential decree. Gerardo Murillo—the future "Dr. Atl"—was their animator. On July 18 he wrote to Director Rivas Mercado asking him for the use of "the class-room of first year of architecture, the exhibition hall, and the corridors of the second floor, to make possible the exhibition that the Society [of Mexican Painters and Sculptors] has planned for the Centennial Year."

Not only did Rivas Mercado allow the young patriots to use

the school building but he contributed 300 pesos out of his own pocket toward expenses. Moved by this example, Secretary of Education Don Justo Sierra added a subvention of 3,000 pesos.

Hung without fanfare in the corridors of the school, this "Show of Works of National Art" overshadows in retrospect the more showy display of Spanish painting. In the Academy show, racial consciousness anticipated the creation of a truly Mexican style. Saturnino Herrán exhibited "The Legend of the Volcanoes," after an Indian myth. Jorge Enciso contributed "Anáhuac" (Fig. 40), a life-size Indian silhouetted against the dawn. One senses justified pride in the thanks that the association sent Rivas Mercado at the close of the show: "The signers, members of the Society of Mexican Painters and Sculptors, are deeply grateful for the active and great goodwill with which you helped us realize this first exhibition of National Art."

To thank Gerardo Murillo further for his management of the show, the artists celebrated with a "victory" dinner held in Santa Anita. There must have been more than soft drinks to go with the hot chili dishes, if we may judge from a news photograph of gesticulating artists hoisting a beaming bearded Murillo onto their swaying shoulders, with Orozco at the bottom of the pile, facing the camera and squinting at the sun.

The fall of Porfirio Díaz—after a semibenevolent dictatorship that lasted nearly forty years—happened soon after the Centennial festivities. His victorious opponent, Francisco I. Madero, made a triumphal entry into the capital in mid-1911, bowing to cheering crowds from a landau drawn by white percherons and manned by liveried coachmen. Art students, eager to taste of the new-found political freedom, lustily injected unrest into the sedate routine of the sheltered Academy. The students' strike, begun in 1911, mirrored in its small

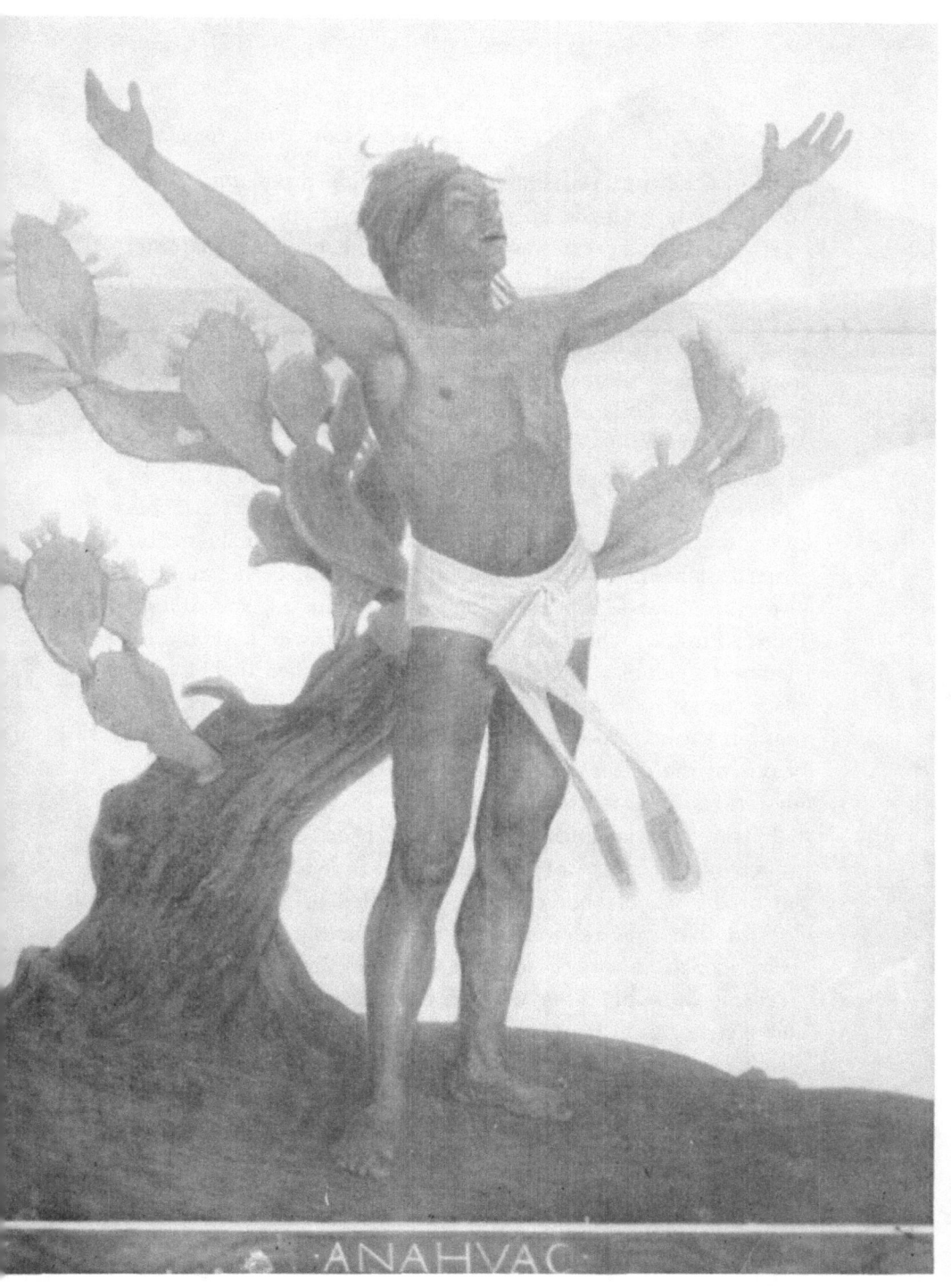

ANAHVAC

FIGURE 40. Jorge Enciso: "Anáhuac." 1910. (Photograph by courtesy of the artist.)

violences the confused and courageous happenings that in the country at large made up the great Revolution.

At first, the unrest was limited to the class of anatomy, taught by Señor Daniel Vergara Lope. His students objected to his dictatorial leanings, at variance with the novel political trend. They rebelled at having to buy from the instructor the mimeographed sheets that served as makeshift textbooks, comparing them disdainfully with the pennysheets of publisher Vanegas Arroyo (see Fig. 41), whose pious and horrendous broadsides were printed on a hand press only a stone's throw from the Academy. The Director arranged a conference between teacher and students to air complaints and make peace. Instead of being conciliatory, Don Daniel called the students —to their face—"beetles, illiterates, effeminates, and starvelings." Enraged, the students formed in answer a syndicate, "Union of Painters and Sculptors," and dispatched their lobbyists to newspapers and various Ministries. Another news photograph shows Orozco standing patiently in the antechamber of one of the upper dogs of the day, a portfolio bulging with mysterious documents under his arm.

In previous troubles, students had been urged to attend classes. Now a squad of policemen had orders to throw them out of the school bodily if they attempted to get in. With a flourish that won reporters and news photographers over to their side, the uncowed students re-formed ranks outside the Academy building. They planted their easels in public parks, and sketched and painted what they saw with a zeal they had rarely felt when inside the school. What they saw and what they painted were people in motion, and landscapes drenched in sunlight filtered through green foliage. Thus a breath of impressionism—modern enough for the Americas and the year 1911—threatened the reign of bitumen shadows inherited from the nineteenth-century Nazarenes.

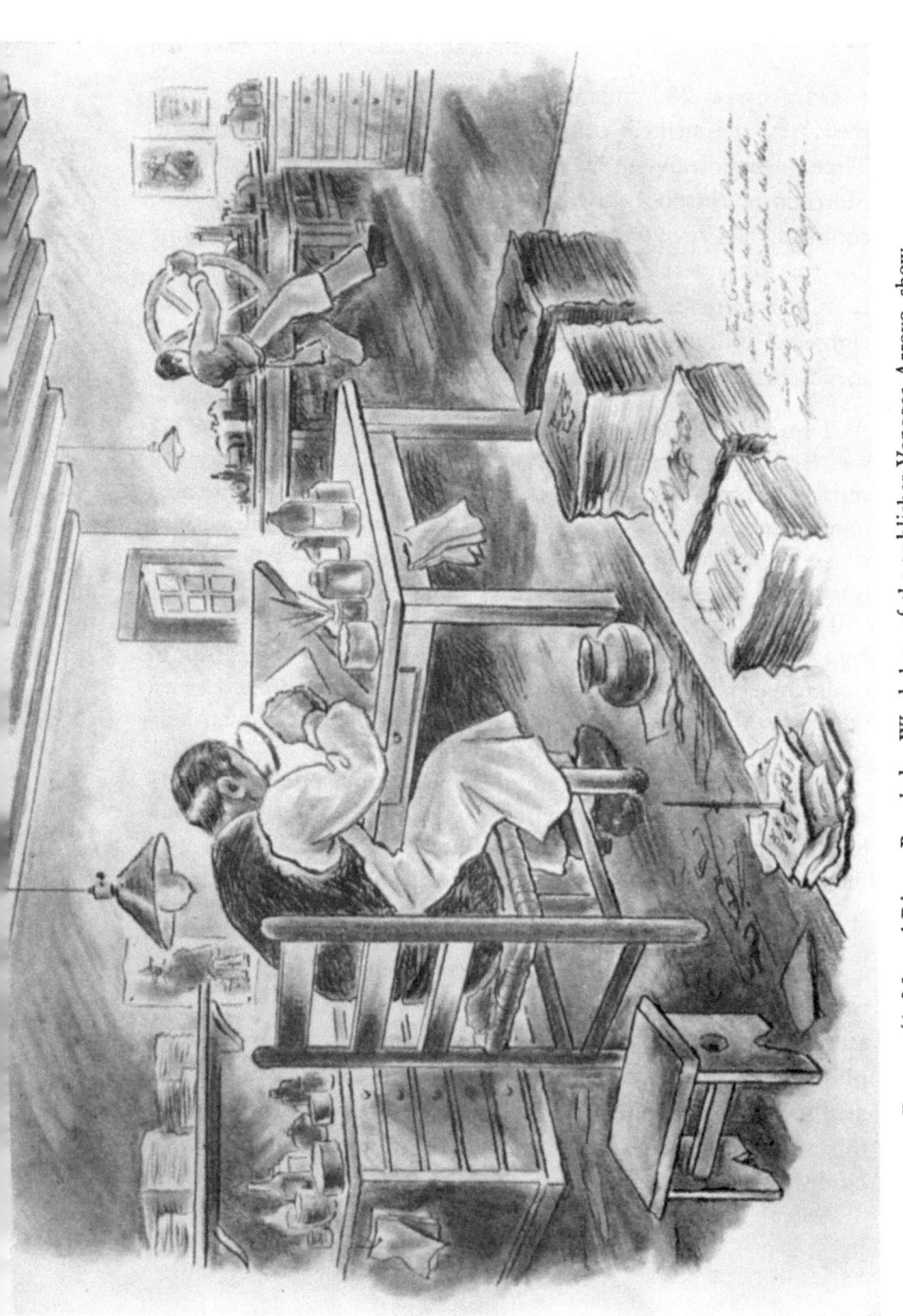

FIGURE 41. Manuel Rivera Regalado: Workshop of the publisher Vanegas Arroyo, showing Guadalupe Posada at his engraver's table. Drawn from memory. (Photograph by Guy Burgess.)

On August 28, undaunted by increasingly forceful police measures, the strikers committed mayhem upon the Director. Though handicapped by both his age and his girth, Rivas Mercado withstood the assault with gallantry, if not with coolness. His own version of the affray, set down that same day for his superior, Secretary of Education Don Justo Sierra, is in the archives. It is a first draft, scrawled in the heat of righteous indignation and filled with erasures and corrections meant to preserve dignity in the midst of mild ridicule:

As I reached, this noon, the Institution, together with my lady, I was faced by a group of malcontents who voiced threats and insults. Far from intimidated, I descended from my automobile, and immediately was attacked by the strikers. They hurled varied missiles—eggs, tomatoes, stones, and other things. One of the objects hit me on the nose, producing a nosebleed.

Thus under attack, I advanced toward the group, my objective being to catch one of them. This I managed to do in the person of troublemaker Francisco Rangel. The rest scattered, and I proceeded on foot to the second police precinct, with a policeman who held Rangel. . . .

While in the street, they continued proffering insults, notwithstanding the presence of my wife, who followed me in the automobile. The chauffeur was manhandled and a striker, wrenching free the hood of one of the headlights, threw it at my wife inside the automobile. . . .

David Alfaro Siqueiros, today rated among Mexican muralists as one of the "three great ones" was present, aged thirteen. He wistfully states that he was scarcely big enough to play a role in the strike: "All I did was to throw a few stones at things and at people, and little else." Somewhat at odds with this self-effacing modesty, however, is the fact that Siqueiros landed in jail that day with some of the ring leaders.

The strike was still on when, eight months after the affray, stubborn Rivas Mercado resigned.

President Madero was shot in 1913, to the benefit of General Huerta, who seated himself in the vacated Presidential Chair. This bad man did more for the good of the Academy than good man Madero ever had. In an election freely held among both teachers and students, the candidate of the anti-Academy element within the school won the directorship of painting. It was under Director Alfredo Ramos Martínez that a new generation of artists would grow to maturity, among them future muralists Alfaro Siqueiros, Revueltas, and Ramón Alva de la Canal. At the time of his election, Ramos Martínez' style of painting, courting Whistler and the post-Impressionists, carried for the young students all the impact of a revolutionary manifesto. Regardless of a style that the artist himself would shed, it proved of crucial importance for the generation of Siqueiros that the new Director thought in terms of a Mexican art, and strived to put his students in daily contact with Mexican subject matter. Thus the long strike begun in 1911 ended victoriously in 1913. The event was signalized by a banquet in honor of Ramos Martínez. On the invitation preserved in the book of clippings of Raziel Cabildo, one of the strike leaders, there is a manuscript notation, "At this fiesta, in a state of absolute drunkenness, Arnulfo S. Domínguez Bello featured in a belly dance." This bacchanalian scene tolled the knell of the old Academy in this year that enthusiasts referred to as the third "Year of Freedoms."

In a letter to the Secretary of Education, dated September, 29, 1913, Ramos Martínez spelled out his aims for the school. Though imbued with the same gentleness that characterized his actions, this text constitutes a truly revolutionary manifesto against the ingrained attitude of local art-lovers who advocated an increased dependency on recognized European masters, men of the caliber of Gérôme, Roybet, and of course Meissonier:

It is the wish of the Direction of the Academy that its students of painting work from the model and in direct contact with nature, in locations where the foliage and perspective effects are true to the character of our *patria.*

The aim is to awaken the enthusiasm of the students for the beauty of our own land, and to give birth to an art worthy of being truthfully called a national art. . . .

Acting on this premise, Ramos Martínez asked from the Secretary permission to take students away from the twilight of the Academy classrooms, and into the sunlight of the countryside. Obviously the chance happenings of the past strike— the lockout of the school against the strikers and their forced contact with the open air—had left indelible marks.

Permission was obtained and a lease was signed on October 17 for a house and garden on the outskirts of Mexico City: "The Direction of the National Academy of Fine Arts is renting a house situated at No. 25, Hidalgo Street . . . in the village of Santa Anita Ixtapalapa. It includes dining room, bedroom, front room, hall, and garden. A class of painting is to be installed there, making possible the direct study from nature. . . . The monthly rental is to be 30.00 pesos."

Thus was started the now historically-famous school of Santa Anita, forerunner of the many open-air schools that were to flourish in Mexico during the 1920's. This "school without walls" was dubbed "Barbizon," to underline the rustic character of the surroundings. Muralist Fernando Leal wrote in his reminiscences of the place:

I had peeked at the classes of the Academy [before Ramos Martínez' time]. The half-begun pictures seemed sordid and the

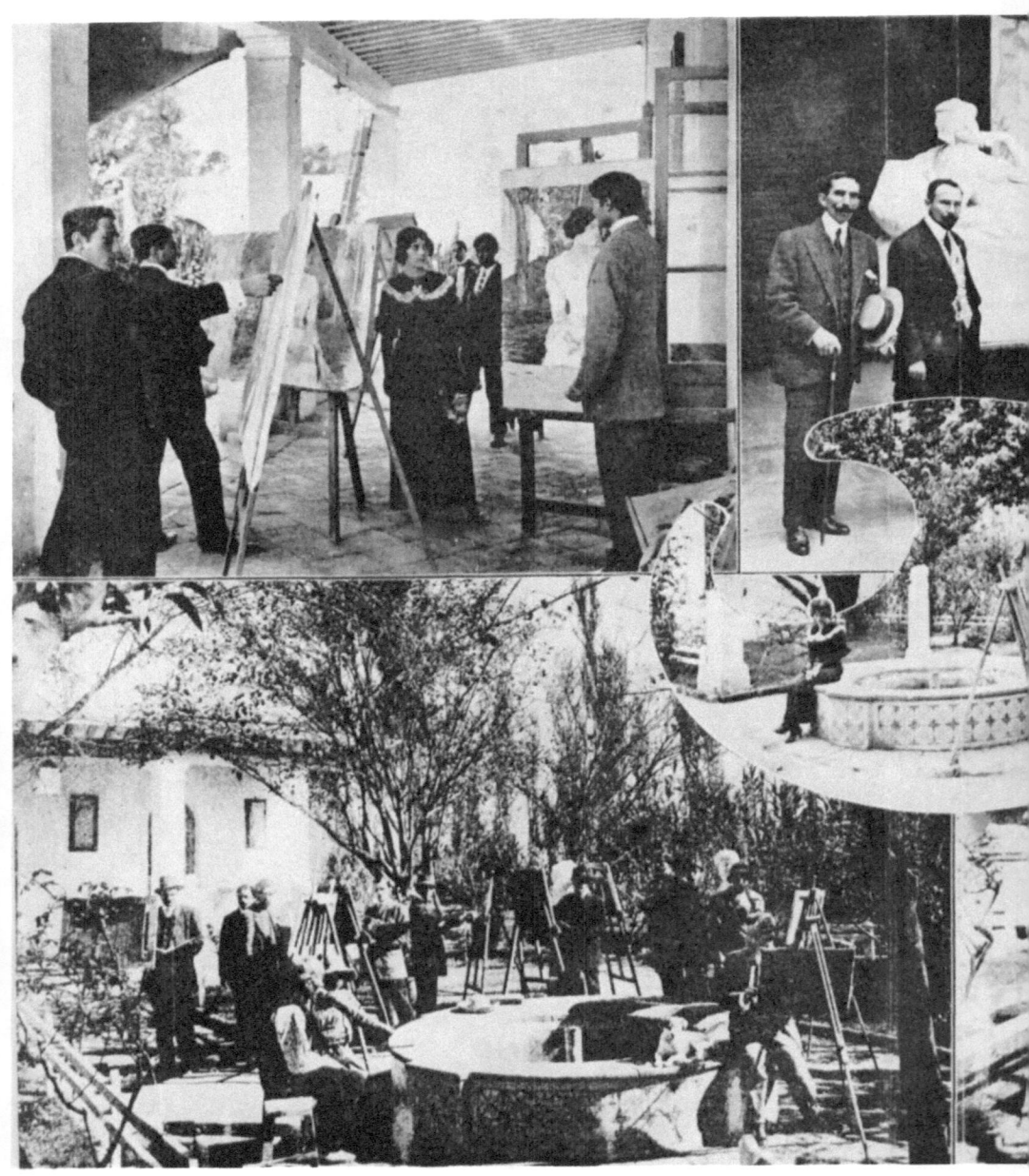

FIGURE 42. Photographs of Barbizon in Santa graphed for *Novedades* by Gardūno.

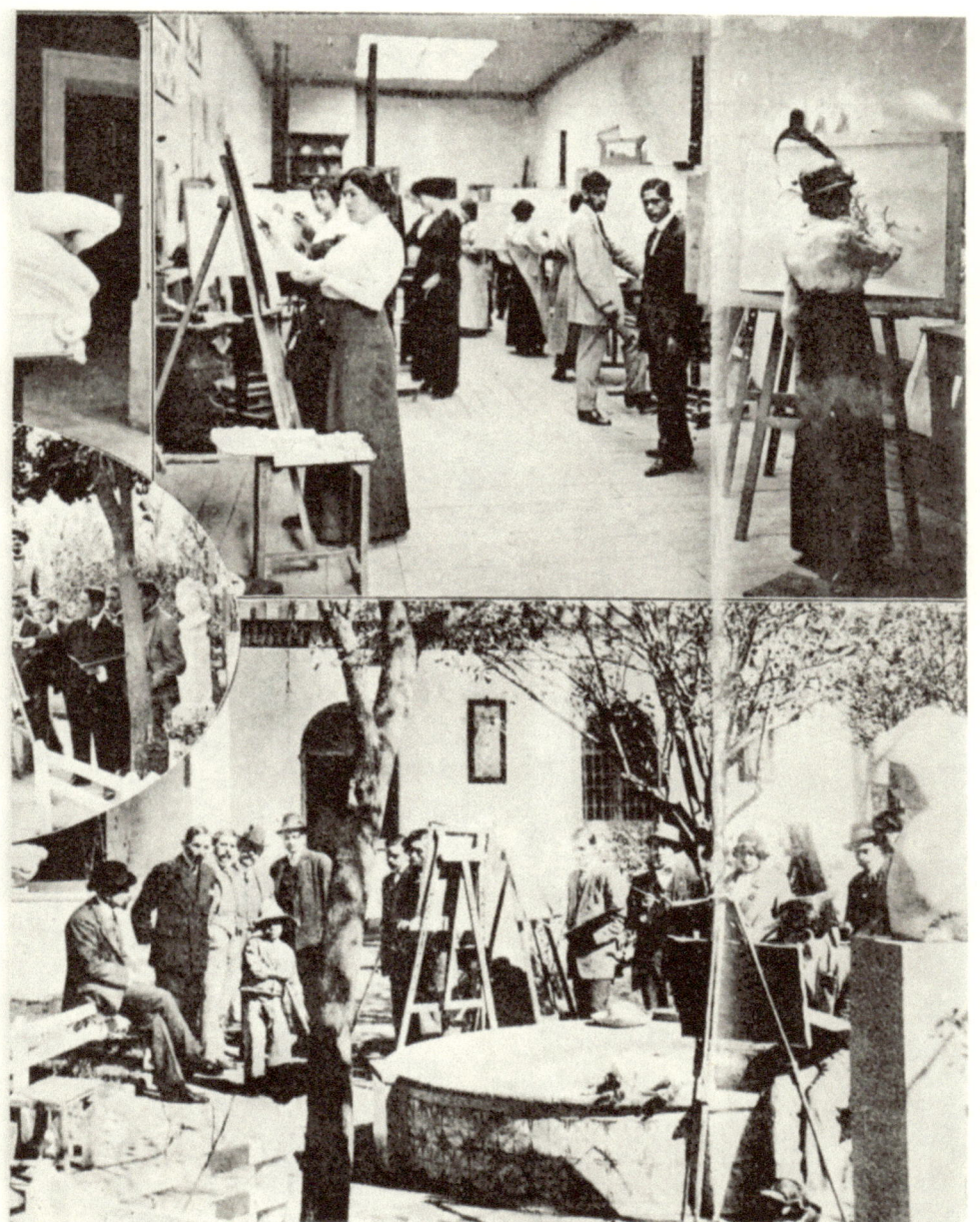

Anita. *Novedades*, June 10, 1914. Photo-

students sunk in greasy *laissez faire.* They played at *Vie de Bohême,* grew long hair, and sang melancholy songs while plucking their guitars in the twilight of the classroom. . . . To visit Santa Anita was by contrast a revelation. . . . Director Ramos Martínez was a gentleman who wore spats and gloves and discussed art exclusively. . . . He punctuated his endless disquisitions with elegant gestures and French expressions, but the overflowing youthful enthusiasm was catching.

The students were the same ones who had disoriented me in the dark buildings of San Carlos, but the open-air light transfigured them. I felt such enthusiasm for their mystical intents at impressionism that I asked to be allowed to paint. To my intense surprise I was given an enormous canvas . . . and a set of colors, minus black and the black-listed earth colors. . . . This was my first picture. I marveled at the confidence shown in me, as materials were handed out without my having attended any class of drawing or of painting, or even being an enrolled student of the school. My model was a woman dressed in rose-hued silk and bathed in the light and reflected lights of a rustic village garden. I started painting as if it were a game and soon heard behind me the exclamations that Ramos Martínez never denied anyone: "It is a Cézanne! One should paint like that without *parti-pris.* What color! Silvery! And *la pâte!* To what texture it builds!" I could understand only a few of these breathless sayings, but I will always remain grateful to Alfredo Ramos Martínez for having confronted me with the most fantastic problems that a painter can face, without attempting to humble me with the pedantry of an academic teacher.

Photographs of Santa Anita's Barbizon (Fig. 42) show easels set up around the chipped blue-tiled fountain in the center of the open patio. Plaster casts transferred there from the storerooms of the Academy vied in attractiveness with live Indian models, and all were set against a natural backdrop of upright poplars mirrored in the shimmering waters of the canal.

At Barbizon, Orozco made a weak attempt at landscape painting, but the setting is linked with names from a younger generation—Leal, from whose recollections we have just read, and Siqueiros. Twofold were the recorded activities of the latter. His schoolmates still speak of his ravening adolescent appetite that led him to Machiavellian plots: he would exalt loudly the esthetic virtues of still-life painting, specifically the rendering of fruits and sundry other edibles. Then, often without waiting for his colleague to finish the picture, Siqueiros would borrow and stealthily devour the models. Not denying this, the artist prefers to tell how, under the cloak of protection spread by the gentle unworldliness of Ramos Martínez, there were underground political meetings at Barbizon, where plots were hatched against the dictatorial Huerta regime.

Barbizon lasted only a few months. With or without the help of its youthful plotters, First Chief Carranza ousted General Huerta, who fled into a California exile. Esthetic fortunes followed political fortunes, and gentle Ramos Martínez was replaced as director of the Academy by Dr. Atl. Having already helped the generation of Orozco and Rivera to an understanding of greatness in the arts, Dr. Atl now endeavored to train the younger men to his heroic concepts. He could hardly stomach the pleasant atmosphere of Barbizon, with its pretty Indian maidens patiently holding pots to their hips or balancing lacquer *bateas* on their heads, and he was even less pleased with the palettes loaded with rainbow hues that Ramos Martínez favored. He would make or break the young students along no less than cosmic lines: "Operative from this date, and valid until countermanded, there will be no more live models in this school.—Mexico, September 12, 1914. . . . Dr. Atl."

If holding the directorship of the school meant having access to the Academy building, Dr. Atl's tenure lasted an even

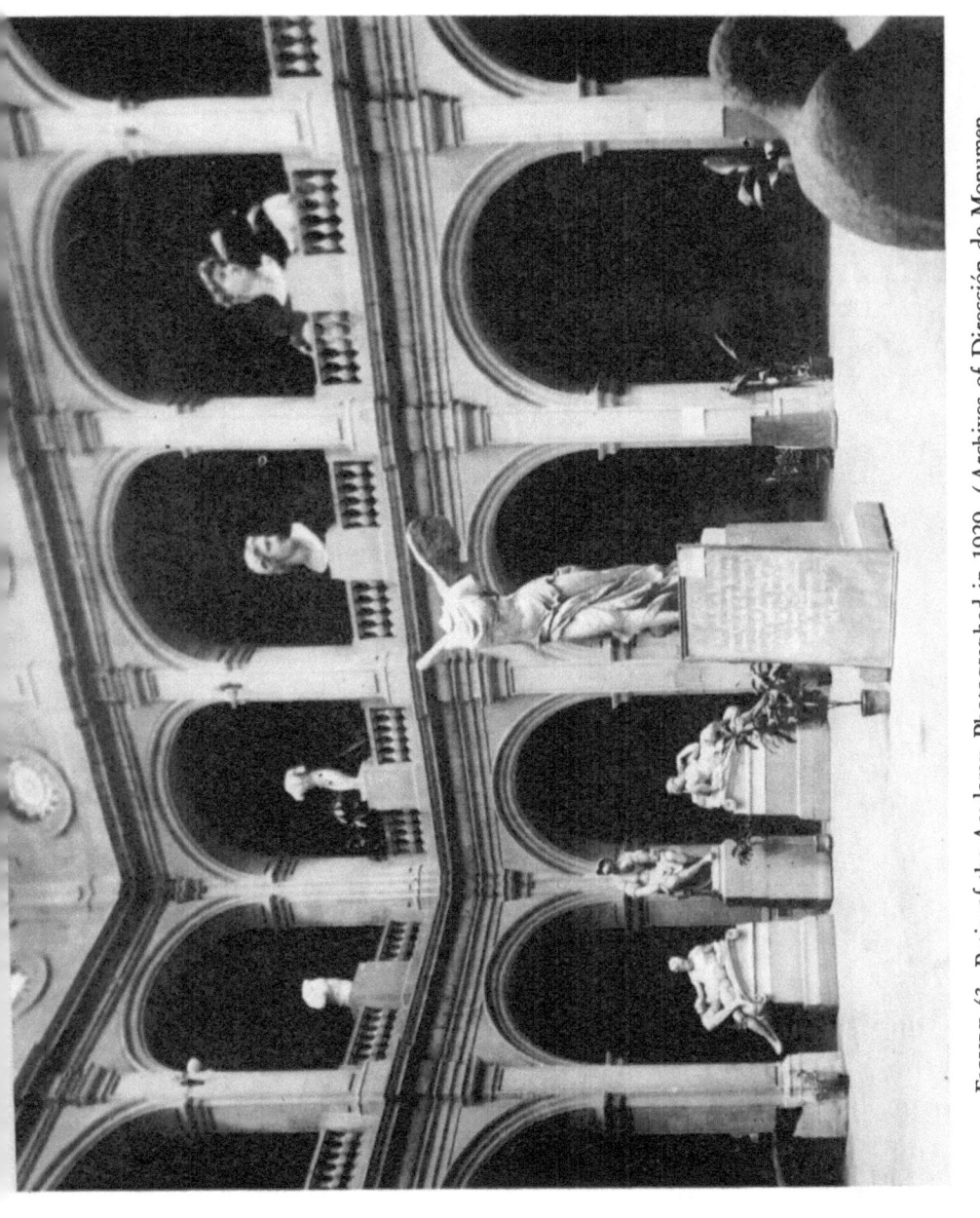

FIGURE 43. Patio of the Academy. Photographed in 1929. (Archives of Dirección de Monumentos Coloniales.)

shorter time than that of Ramos Martínez. It would be more exact to say that, when Pancho Villa entered Mexico City and beaten Carranza holed up in provincial Orizaba, Dr. Atl installed there an Academy in exile. This political move had even more far-reaching repercussions on the future of Mexican art than did the lockout of students during the 1911–1913 strike. In Orizaba, it was not the pleasant sights of city parks that met the eye of the young painters. Here they came face to face with the bleeding form of their torn *patria,* a re-enactment in true and live tableaux of the kind of episodes Spanish Goya had etched a century before. Dr. Atl, a staunch foe of art for art's sake, saw to it that the students missed nothing of the horrors that were a daily fare. Carranza mostly fought the agrarian hordes of Zapata. A daily batch of prisoners—Indian farmers turned warriors, in white *calzones* and wide-brimmed hats—was brought in from the battlefields and shot in the city square in the early dawn. The sacked church, which was to the artists a combination dormitory, studio, and pressroom, faced that square. It was Orozco's job to toll the church bells to call his colleagues to breakfast. Presumably, it was the dawn shootings that awoke him in turn.

Siqueiros felt quite at ease with this strong fare. Longing for more than a sideline contact with the battlefields, he soon left for forthright military pursuits, the youngest officer on the staff of General Diéguez, steady foe of Villa. The painter proved to be a good soldier, and his companions-in-arms considered art his only weakness. Once, when Siqueiros offered to sketch General Diéguez, the crusty old man exploded, "I refuse to have my photograph taken by a boy still wet behind the ears!"

Eventually, the Academy of San Carlos, become the National School of Art, was to return to a routine life and a daily round of art classes conducted in the classrooms of its ancient building. With the hindsight that is called historical perspective, one realizes that the revolutionary period 1910–1915, marked by a physical dissolution of the comforts and order associated with a school, is nevertheless one of the most vital moments in the long history of the Academy. It parallels that other period around 1840, when rent and salaries were unpaid, and the school ready to close, when a ferment of *mexicanidad* pitted the students, with Mata at their head, against a despairing Board of Trustees.

It could be argued, as is so often done, that the ultimate result of the existence of the Academy of San Carlos has been to slow up the development of a national style. I rather believe that, by providing a locus where the young could be taught, where the older artist was assured of a living, and by acting as a showcase for living art, the Academy's role has been beneficial. One can even argue that, in the periods when the Academy was most strictly run along academic lines, it helped the young, by contrast, to realize the meaning of freedom. When the school was manned by men blind to the Mexican tradition, and sensitive only to European values, their stubborn stand became a most healthy invitation to artistic revolution. One thing is certain, the history of Mexican art cannot be dissociated from the history of the school founded in 1785 as the Royal Academy of San Carlos of New Spain.

INDEX

Academia de Virtuosi al Panteon (Rome): Juan Cordero member of, 98 n.

Académico de Mérito: accessibility of, to Indians, 54; Pedro Patiño Ixtolinque's application for, 60–64

academies, art: in Spanish America, 10

academies, European: influence of upon Academy, 25, 28–30

Academy of San Carlos: Neo-Classicism in, 9, 88, 90; archives of, 10; history of, 10, 19; and Mexican history, 12; present nature of, 19, 20; doctrine of, 20; original drawings at, 20; statutes of, 24, 26 n.; curriculum of, 25–28, 79; directors of, 25, 28–30, 33, 40, 44, 60, 70, 75–76, 76–78, 103, 122, 125, 132, 134–136, 142, 144, 159, 162; organization of, 26; teachers at, 33, 103; and Fernando José Mangino, 36; race relations in, 53–55, 60–64; finances of, 65, 67–68, 78, 102–103; and revolutions, 65–68, 144, 154, 162, 164, 165; and liberal Spanish constitution, 65–66; and national independence, 66–67; closing of, 67; and Governing Board, 68; "dark ages" of, 69; and National Lottery, 69, 101, 125, 128; salaries paid by, 78 n.–79 n.; suit against, 84; reorganization of, 85,

Coghetti: painting by, 98 n.; candidate for director of Academy of San Carlos, 103

Colonial period: in Mexican art, 9

"Columbus before the Catholic Sovereigns": by Juan Cordero, 86, 98–99

Column of Independence in Paseo de la Reforma: by Antonio Rivas Mercado, 144

Comonfort, General Ignacio: and General Santa Anna, 119

constitution, liberal Spanish: and King Ferdinand, 66

Contreras, Mariano: in lithography studio, 75

Contreras (forename unknown): drawing by, 88, 90

Cordero, Juan: biography of, 86, 93; "Columbus before the Catholic Sovereigns" by, 86, 98–99; and Honorato Riano, 93, 96; and Primitivo Miranda, 93, 96, 100; in Rome, 93–95, 95–96, 96–98, 99; and Academy of San Carlos, 93 n.–95 n., 95–96, 118–120; and General Bustamante, 94; Francisco Zarco on, 94, 100; pensions received by, 95–96; Carlos París on, 96; and Cavallero Carta, 96; to Manuel de Bonilla, 98; in Academia de Virtuosi al Panteon, 98 n.; attacks against, 99–100; "The Redeemer and the Woman Taken in Adultery" by, 100, 116–118; return to Mexico, 100 n.; and Pelegrin Clavé, 100 n., 144; *La Ilustración Mexicana* on, 116–118; and General Santa Anna, 118, 119; murals by, 122

Cornelius, Peter von: director of Prussion Academy (Rome), 103; influence of, on Pelegrin Clavé, 106; and Santiago Rebull, 140

Cortés, Hernando: in cartoon, 138

costumes: use of, in teaching drawing, 146

Costumes du Mexique: by Claudio Linati, 75

Couto, José Bernardo: on Joseph de Alzíbar, 32; on Ginés de Andrés y de Aguirre, 34 n.; and Academy of San Carlos, 110; *Diálogo* by, 110; petition of, 119

crafts: Indian in, 50

Creole teachers: 30, 144

Culture: efforts to achieve, 11

David, Jacques Louis: influence on Claudio Linati, 72; mentioned, 10

Da Vinci, Leonardo: influence of, on Clavé, 106

Dehesa, Teodoro: and Diego Rivera, 152

Delaroche, Paul: influence of, on Clavé, 106

Diálogo: by José Bernardo Couto, 110

Díaz, Porfirio: and Academy of San Carlos, 134; and Antonio Fabrés, 144; and celebration of Mexican Centennial Year, 153; fall of, 154

Diéguez, General: and David Alfaro Siqueiros, 164

dies, casting. *See* casting dies

discrimination: against native artists, 30, 91, 92, 99–100, 103

Domínguez Bello, Arnulfo S.: at party for Alfredo Ramos Martínez, 159

drawing, teaching of: in curriculum, 25–26; use of plaster casts in, 56 n.–58 n.; photography in, 146; use of costumes in, 146

drawings, original: at Academy of San Carlos, 20; signatures on, 46 n.

"Drinkers, The": by Diego Velázquez, 144

Echave, Balthazar de: and Mexican art, 32

Echeverría, Javier: and Academy of San Carlos, 102; and National Lottery, 102

Egypt: art in, 11

Enciso, Jorge: "Anáhuac" by, 154

Index

www.ingramcontent.com/pod-product-compliance
Lightning Source LLC
Chambersburg PA
CBHW031048180526
45163CB00002BA/734